How to Draw and Paint with your Computer

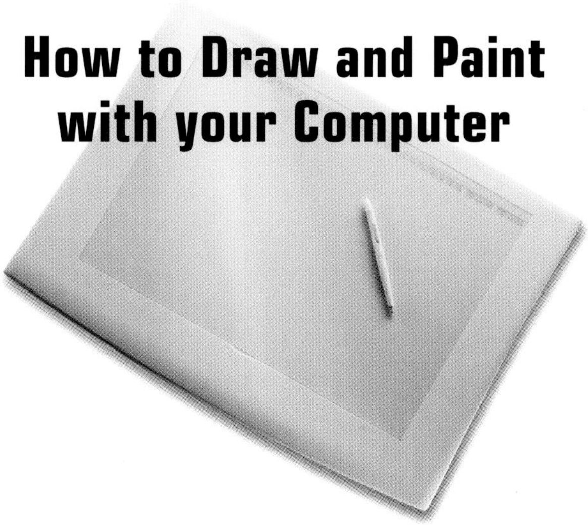

How to Draw and Paint with your Computer

Glen Wilkins

HarperCollins*Publishers*

A QUARTO BOOK

First published in 2000 by
HarperCollins*Publishers*
77–85 Fulham Palace Road
Hammersmith
London W6 8JB

Collins is a registered trademark of
HarperCollins Publishers Ltd

The HarperCollins website address is
www.**fire**and**water**.com

05 04 03 02 01 00
9 8 7 6 5 4 3 2 1

A catalogue record for this book is available from the British Library

ISBN 0-00-413406-0

QUAR.HOW

Conceived, designed and produced by
Quarto Publishing plc
The Old Brewery
6 Blundell Street
London N7 9BH

EDITOR Sarah Vickery
DESIGNER Luise Roberts
ASSISTANT ART DIRECTOR Penny Cobb
INDEXER Diana LeCore

ART DIRECTOR Moira Clinch
PUBLISHER Piers Spence

Manufactured by Regent Publishing Services Ltd, Hong Kong

Printed by Leefung-Asco Printers Ltd, China

Dedication

For Lesley Catherine, my love

Contents

Introduction

Is digital artwork a valid and justifiable artform? It's a question that arises again and again. Perhaps the people who ask this question are scared of technology. Perhaps they feel that the computer will rob them of their creative spark, and the reason behind making art. Nothing could be further from the truth. Whatever the medium or means of creation, art conveys an artist's idea. The desire to inform, stimulate or decorate still has to come from within.

Creating artwork with your computer is inspirational and exciting. Digital technology lends itself to experimentation: you can try out new media and different surfaces without having to worry about the cost of paints and papers. And discovering techniques that are simply not possible with conventional art materials can be a revelation.

'I bet Leonardo would have rushed out and bought an iMac and Wacom Tablet.'

Traditionally, art has been the foil to science, but the new digital era has brought these two disparate fields together. Computer generated art is created with pure mathematics and heralds a new era of artistic freedom. Today's Internet galleries take art to a worldwide audience, even making it possible for artists on opposite sides of the world to collaborate on the same work.

I believe the artist should view the computer as just another tool. Although this book aims to help you imitate traditional painting and drawing media I hope that it will be a springboard for new ideas and techniques that do not have a real media equivalent.

Enjoy...

GLEN WILKINS
Spinal Crack
1999

XRES

Photoshop

Illustrator

PhotoDeluxe

Painter

Art Dabbler

ColorIt

CorelDRAW

CorelPAINT

LivePIX

FreeHand

How to use this book

The book is divided into three sections, which together explain everything you need to know about painting with pixels. It presents the theory and practice behind a range of traditional art techniques applied in a completely new way.

The first chapter introduces you to the equipment and software needed to begin making digital art. With your studio in place, Digital Tools explains the basic principles of creating computer art. Each medium is then explored in turn, with step-by-step demonstrations and expert tips designed to help you get the most from your computer.

The second chapter will give you the opportunity to put your new-found skills into practice. Imaginative projects employ a range of advanced techniques to inspire you further.

Once your artwork is complete, turn to Getting Technical for advice on transferring your masterpiece from screen to page.

HEADING
The heading indicates whether the spread covers tablet or plug-in techniques

ICONS
These appear at the side of each page and highlight suitable programs

TECHNIQUE SWATCHES
A range of basic techniques is demonstrated

54 DIGITAL TOOLS: DRAWING

Oil pastel with a tablet

Oil pastels are dense in texture, with the oil base giving the medium viscosity and adding substance to the marks made on the paper or canvas. It is possible to blend colours with great subtlety, giving flexibility and control. However, the medium also lends itself to working quickly, sketching in areas of colour and tone, with detail being added later with fine pastels or pencil.

Stylus pressure
The pastel marks become heavier and denser by varying the pressure on the stylus. Oil pastel tends to fill-in when used heavily, with little paper grain showing through.

Smudging
Oil pastel can be blended by smudging line work with a finger or torchon. The digital artist can simulate this effect by using a wet brush to move and soften marks.

Working on textured papers
Experiment with creating paper texture using pastels, or try working with a limited palette of colours and using a tinted base paper.

Blending
Using short, controlled marks it is possible to create gradual colour changes. The colour was changed from red to yellow and blended by varying through a range of oranges.

Crosshatching
Crosshatching techniques work effectively with all pastels and are an easy and effective way of laying in large areas of tone.

Pointillist
Optical colour mixing occurs when short marks or dots are used to create a pattern and it is left to the viewer's eye to decipher the image.

Soft tones
A large, soft brush with little pressure applied to the stylus simulates the effects of using the side of a pastel stick.

Heavy pastel marks
The digital artist can simulate depth by working with vibrant or opposing colours and running a Lighting filter to define areas where colours meet.

DETAIL
Glass objects can be made to look three-dimensional by the careful placing of highlights. On rounded objects, such as this bottle, the light bouncing off the glass should follow the contours of the form and have a diffused edge.

The icons on each spread indicate which software can be used to complete the techniques demonstrated.

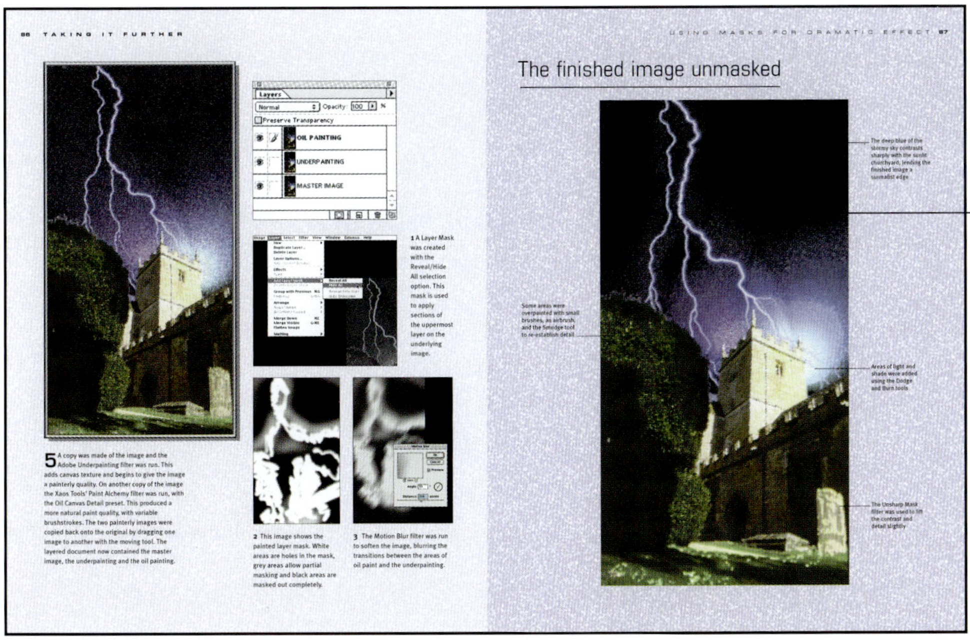

THE FINAL IMAGE
Annotated with additional advice and information to provide the finishing touch

Projects begin with clear objectives and teaching points. They break down image creation into easy-to-follow steps.

CONTROL PANEL
Interface variables and their uses are described

OPTIONS
The many plug-in variables are shown, with notes on how to achieve similar effects

TIPS
Additional ideas to experiment with to bring your artwork to life

What is digital artwork?

Digital artwork can be defined as any image that has been processed by a computer at some stage in its creation. The artwork may have been created digitally or been altered by computer in some way. This definition includes images that have been scanned for print production as posters, books or magazines. The average viewer of printed material has, therefore, been exposed to some form of digital art. However, this book deals solely with artwork that has been created within a computer using paint or image editing software.

IS IT REAL?

The digital artist manipulates a series of pixels to create the illusion of an intellectual idea. The image exists only as a binary string within the computer, a series of 1s and 0s or on/off switches. This image data can be infinitely rearranged, copied and even transferred electronically around the world to other artists or viewers. The idea behind the image has been captured using only maths, and does not exist in the conventional sense of paint on canvas. So it could be argued that until the image is printed it does not exist and is, therefore, not real.

REALIZING THE PROJECT

Computer software has evolved to the point where the painter or sketcher can work with the digital equivalent of most traditional painting and drawing media. But why would an artist want to work with computer tools that merely replicate conventional materials? The answer lies in the many advantages of working digitally.

The techniques and working practices of the digital painter can lead to greater experimentation, as the speed at which work is created allows the artist to try out several different versions of the image. Composition, colour and even painting medium can be varied until the desired results are achieved. The tools used will never run out of paint or be blunted, offer unlimited colour choice, and the ability to erase any mistakes at the press of a button. The artwork can be saved as each stage is completed, giving the painter the

KATIE HAYDEN, Self Promotion, using Photoshop.

DONALD GAMBINO, using Photoshop.

PHILIP NICHOLSON, using Painter.

KEN RAMEY, using Photoshop plug-ins.

BRIAN WILKINS, George Lazenby, using Painter.

opportunity to retrace his steps and rework an image. Digital painting tools also allow the painter to try out techniques that would be impossible with traditional paints and brushes. These include working with mixed media, such as placing watercolour over an oil painting.

More commissioned illustration and artwork is being created digitally. This is often dictated by time and economic factors: publishers don't have to wait for paints to dry and the cost of having real artwork scanned is avoided.

The major drawback for the digital painter is in the way that artwork is created: all contact with real paint, brushes or canvas is lost.

THE PLUG-IN FACTOR

Above and beyond new media tools, the computer has an armoury of plug-in tools, which are studied in detail within the Digital Tools section. The plug-in will work within a host program, such as Adobe Photoshop, to create effects that range from simulating real media painting to assisting with the production of digital images.

The most common plug-ins are a range of filters that work within a host program to change an image, or a selection within an image, using variable controls to achieve painterly or stylistic effects. Oil paint, fresco, coloured pencils, photocopy, blur and sharpen are among these filters. In fact, most real media paint techniques have a plug-in equivalent.

Other filters do not attempt to replicate real paint but offer a range of effects that can border on the surreal. Clouds, sparks, stains, fur, plastic wrap, chrome, crumpled paper and distortion filters are just some of many.

Finally, there are filters that help with the production of a digital artwork. These include tools for colour correction, preparing images for professional output via colour separation software and digital portfolio software.

WHAT IS A PIXEL?

The building blocks of the digital artist, pixels are the smallest components of an image. The artist has to manipulate these elements to reveal form or colour within the artwork.

A pixel equates to an individual tile on a tiled wall.

PAUL CROCKWELL, Hind, using Photoshop and Photoimpact.

RANDY SOWASH,
using Photoshop.

KIT MONROE, using Photoshop and Kai's Power Tools.

These tiles can be arranged by colour or tone to create an overall image on the wall. The number of tiles used to create the image directly relates to the quality of the final output – the more tiles used, the greater the detail.

A basic understanding of how many tiles should be used in artwork creation is vital before commencing any work (see Scanning Resolution, page 32). The second important factor when creating an image concerns how much information is contained within one pixel. This directly relates to the image's bit depth, or the colour mode being used. If the wall was covered with only black and white tiles, the image would be formed as line-art. Creating a greyscale image would require tiles ranging from black to white, and covering many shades of grey. A colourful image would need vast numbers of different coloured tiles, increasing the complexity of the image and affecting the working practices of the painter. The digital artist often has to compromise between picture quality and speed of work.

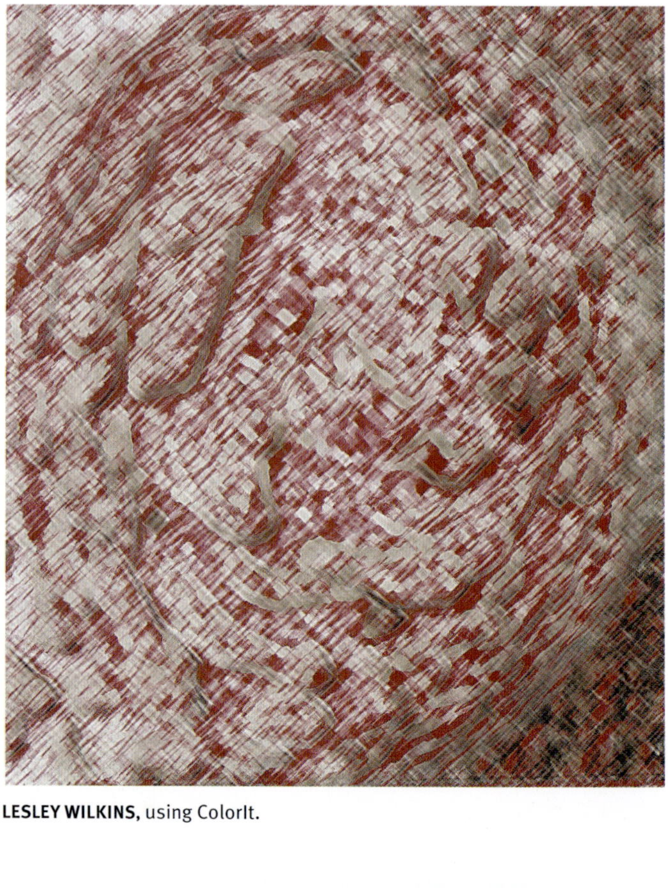

LESLEY WILKINS, using ColorIt.

MAUREEN NAPPI, using Photoshop and Kai's Power Tools.

WENDY GROSSMAN, using Illustrator, Photoshop and Ray Dream Designer.

Building a studio

THE COMPUTER

The first essential purchase that the digital artist must make is the computer processor itself, the CPU. This is the grey box that performs all the processing tasks and enables you to work. Once you have decided on PC or Mac platforms, there are three key elements to look at:

- Processing speed or clock speed
- RAM (random access memory)
- Hard disk space.

The processor

The processor, or main chip within the computer, performs all the key computing tasks. The power of the chip and, therefore, the computer is determined by the chip's clock speed, which relates directly to how fast instructions are carried out, and is measured in megahertz (MHz). The faster the speed, the greater the performance of the computer, which in turn makes digital artworking easier for the user. As paint and imaging software is memory and speed-hungry, the user will notice slower clock speeds: filters can take a long time to process or paint marks can slowly trail behind when using a stylus. It is a good investment to buy the fastest clock speed you can afford: software becomes more advanced and processor-hungry at an alarming rate and processors that seem fast one day soon lag behind and can hinder production.

The standard for PC processors are the Intel Pentium chips. These have been taken on-board by the majority of PC manufacturers, although other brands are

G3's Basic Specification

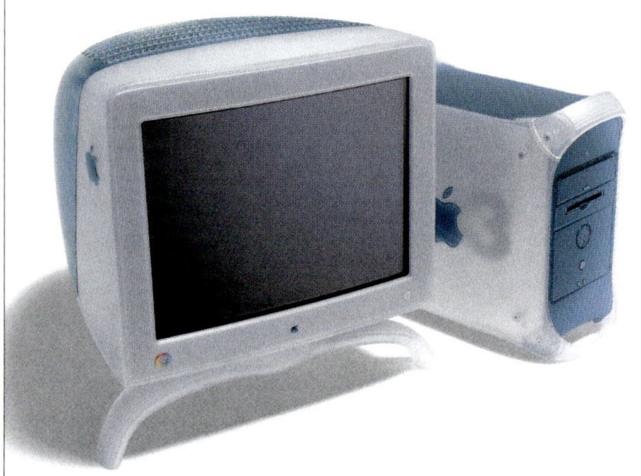

Popular with the design community, the Apple Macintosh G3 Tower runs at clock speeds of between 300 and 450MHz. It has an architecture that allows for upgrading, and is ideal for memory-hungry image manipulation software. It is shown here with the Apple studio display.

Apple iMac
Popular because of its radical looks, the Apple iMac is a very powerful and user-friendly computer. Impressive clock speeds linked to fast hard disks make this machine an ideal candidate for the home digital art studio.

The AP500 from Compaq
An affordable dual-processor professional workstation. The CPU processes digital data via two Pentium II chips, making this an ideal base to build a digital studio.

available that are Intel-compatible. Intel's Pentium III is an effective processor when setting up a studio.

The PowerMac G3 processor, runs at speeds up to 400MHz, although this figure is constantly rising. Note that this chip does not relate to PC speeds, as G3 chips are more powerful and the Mac's internal architecture increases the clock speed beyond the specified speeds. A G3 Mac running with a chip speed of 350MHz, for example, will outperform an Intel Pentium PC running at 400MHz.

RAM

The RAM, or random access memory, relates to the amount of work the computer can do. RAM is used to process data from any programs in use and is measured in megabytes (Mb). The greater the RAM, the more efficient the computer will be. Most computers allow for extra RAM to be fitted and chips can be purchased and simply slotted into the computer. The minimum requirement for running your digital studio would be 64Mb, although you should buy as much RAM as you can afford.

When working on a digital file it is advisable to allocate RAM of between three to five times the file's size, so a 20Mb Photoshop file will need 60 to 100Mb of RAM. A good digital set-up would have a minimum of 128Mb.

Hard disk

Hard disk space is measured in gigabytes (Gb). The hard disk is the amount of computer space available to store work when the machine has been switched off. The greater the number, or the bigger the hard disk, the better the computer. The hard disk can also be used as a type of RAM by some computer softwares. This is known as virtual memory. The software will save part of the digital file onto your hard disk, process the tasks on the remaining file held in RAM, and then call back the file saved to the hard disk. This can lead to image processing taking longer than usual and can even result in files filling the hard disk, leaving the user unable to save work in progress. It is, therefore, sensible to have three times the file size of a working document available on the hard disk.

Again, the price of hard disk space is rapidly falling, with capacity increasing at the same rate. The minimum hard disk size recommended for the studio is 4Gb. However, 6 and 12Gb disks are becoming more affordable so try to buy the biggest available.

Monitors

The monitor, or screen, is the key interface between the computer and the digital artist. Standard sizes for monitors, which are measured across the diagonal, are 15in, 17in, 19in, 20in and 21in. The price of a monitor does not directly relate to the increase in size: a good 20in monitor could easily be double the price of a 17in equivalent.

Most monitors can be 'bundled' with a computer and bought at the same time, reducing the cost to the end user. The standard bundled monitor is 15in, too small for detailed artwork. As with everything else, greater expense will benefit your work. Larger screens make working easier, although the difference will become less apparent between a 20 and 21in.

A less expensive option is to buy two small screens and run both off the same computer. A 15in and 17in monitor gives the artist the digital equivalent of a 32in screen at a fraction of the cost. The two screens can be set up with the artist's tools laid out on the smaller monitor and the painting area on the larger screen.

The monitor is driven by a graphics or video card inside the main computer, which vary in power and speed. The greater the screen redraw and screen resolution, the better the graphics card. When buying a computer and monitor it is important that you check that 'Millions' of colours are available. Lower screen resolutions will be noticeable when working with digital art files, as the range of colours will be limited.

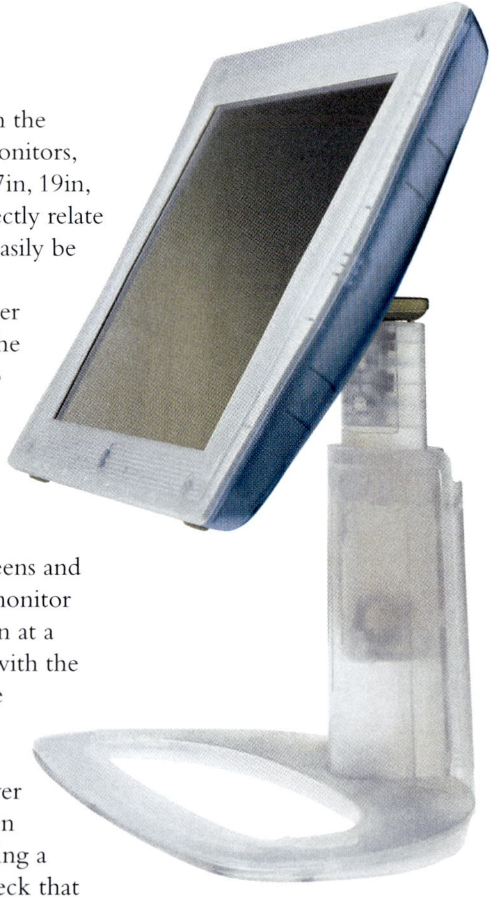

Apple Studio Display
This flat screen uses TFT (Thin Film Transfer) to greatly reduce the amount of desk space it needs. The screen supports high resolution, although the screen redraw is slower than on conventional monitors.

Tablets and stylus

Many artists familiar with working with real pencil and paintbrush will find the mouse an awkward and clumsy drawing tool. The answer is to buy a tablet and stylus. The tablet plugs into the computer and acts as a drawing board. The stylus, or pen, is used as you would a pencil on the drawing board. As you draw on the tablet the mouse pointer on screen will move in the same way, making this a natural drawing tool that does not require the user to learn any new skills.

Graphics tablets range in size from postcard up to A3, and beyond. Larger tablets are obviously easier

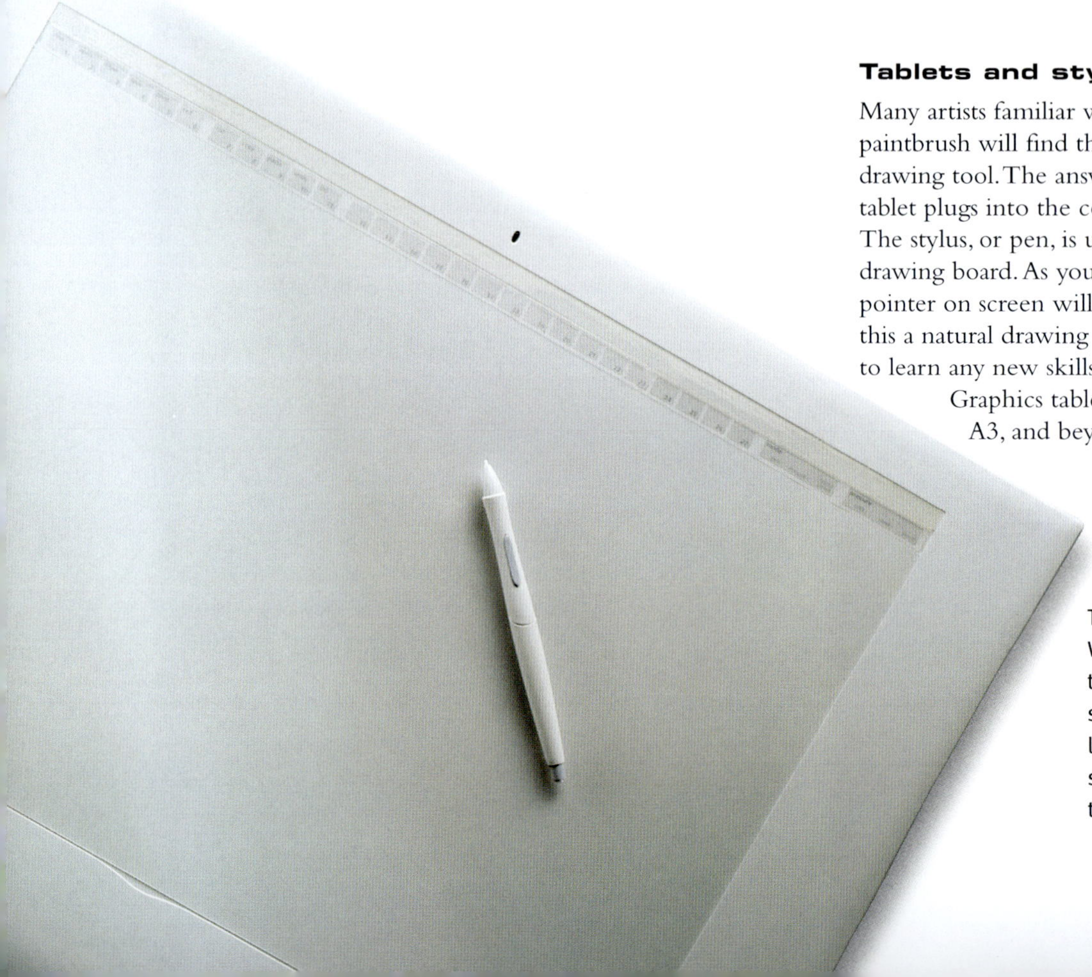

The Intuos range of tablet and stylus from Wacom closely replicates real media tools. Pressure-sensitive variables can be set, with digital brushes producing darker line work when pressure is applied to the stylus. The eraser tool is accessed by turning the stylus upside down.

to use, but bring a dramatic increase in cost. An A5 tablet is usable and affordable, making it a wise investment. Some tablets have a series of programable buttons that can be utilized for repetitive tasks. For example, buttons can be programed to open files, create documents or save work. Most styli also have one or two buttons that can be programed by the user to act as a keyboard command key, such as option or control.

The stylus is pressure sensitive and software can be programed to vary the weight of line, the darkness of the strokes or the colour of the paint. Increased pressure can give thicker lines, and tilting the stylus produces varying brush marks. There are styli available for different purposes, including the Wacom Intuos series with stylus for paint, ink and airbrush.

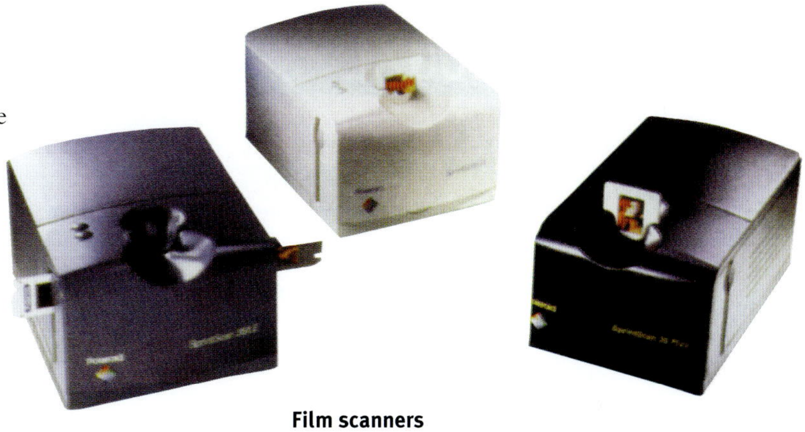

Film scanners
Ideal for scanning 35mm transparencies or negatives, these scanners offer higher resolutions and use less space than desktop scanners.

Scanning devices

Input devices are defined as tools that will capture an image for use on the computer. These include scanners, digital cameras, video cameras (s-video and digital), video grabbers, and tablet and stylus.

The major input device purchase will be a flatbed desktop scanner. These are relatively cheap and are indispensable when working from photographs. They work in a similar way to a photocopier, with the original photograph or transparency laid onto a flat glass plate. A small strip light scans across the original and the information is captured by a chip, called a charged couple device (CCD), which converts the image into computer data that can be opened by image and paint software. Film scanners offer better quality when working with slides or transparencies, although desktop scanners are more versatile. Two factors must be considered when assessing the quality of a scanner: optical resolution and bit depth, or colour depth. Greater optical resolution results in clearer scans, with more detail captured, particularly in shadow areas. Optical resolution is normally measured in dots per inch, with a typical scanner offering 300x600dpi. The colour depth will be measured in bits. An RGB images requires 24 bits, while CMYK requires greater bit depths (see Digital Colour, page 28 and Scanning Resolution, page 32). A compromise must be made between image quality and cost of purchase. If scans are only to be used as reference for artwork, then lower optical resolutions will be acceptable.

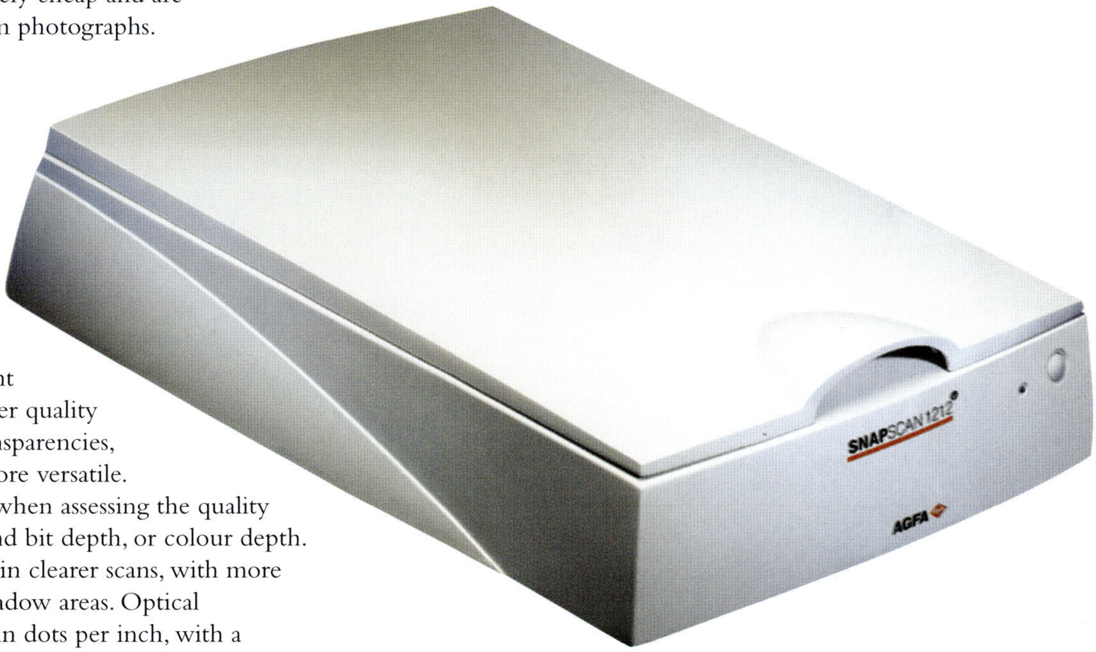

Desktop scanner
This Agfa Snapscan is an affordable, good quality desktop scanner that can be used with both PC and Mac-based systems.

Digital camera
Digital still cameras work in the same way as conventional compact film cameras, but write the image as digital data that can be accessed immediately by the computer. As technology advances, quality is improving, and prices are falling.

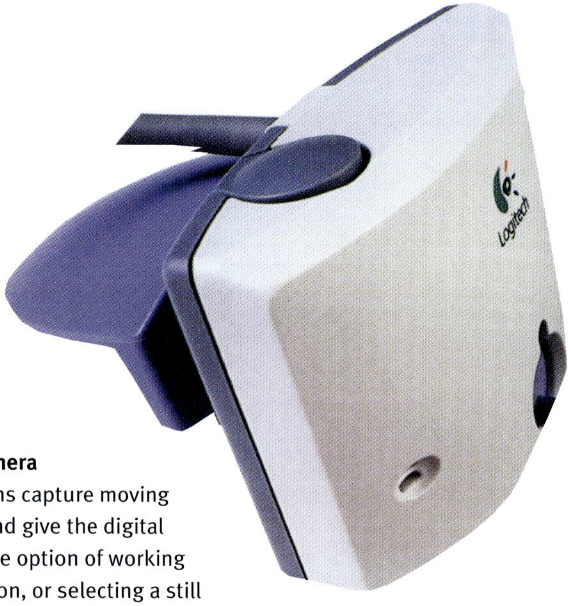

Video camera
Video cams capture moving images and give the digital painter the option of working with motion, or selecting a still image from the information.

Digital cameras

The other main input device for digital artists is the digital camera. These work in the same way as conventional cameras, but images are captured by a built-in CCD. Their obvious advantage over desktop scanners is that they are portable, and are ideal if you want to capture a scene or portrait to be used as the basis for a painting.

Printers

Output devices, such as desktop printers, are becoming readily available, affordable, and have remarkable print quality. Desktop inkjet printers work by squirting tiny dots of ink onto paper, using four or six colors to give very realistic and accurate images. The output resolution of these printers can be as high as 1440dpi, printing to glossy photographic paper produces the best results. Most inkjets are bundled with print management software for greater printing controls. Professional inkjet printing is affordable and available in sizes ranging from A4 to poster.

Color laser printers work in the same way as color photocopiers, with CMYK inks attracted to ordinary carrier paper. The cost of buying this technology, or even using it on a regular basis, can be prohibitive. It is only possible to print up to size A3: anything beyond this has to be tiled to several sheets of paper.

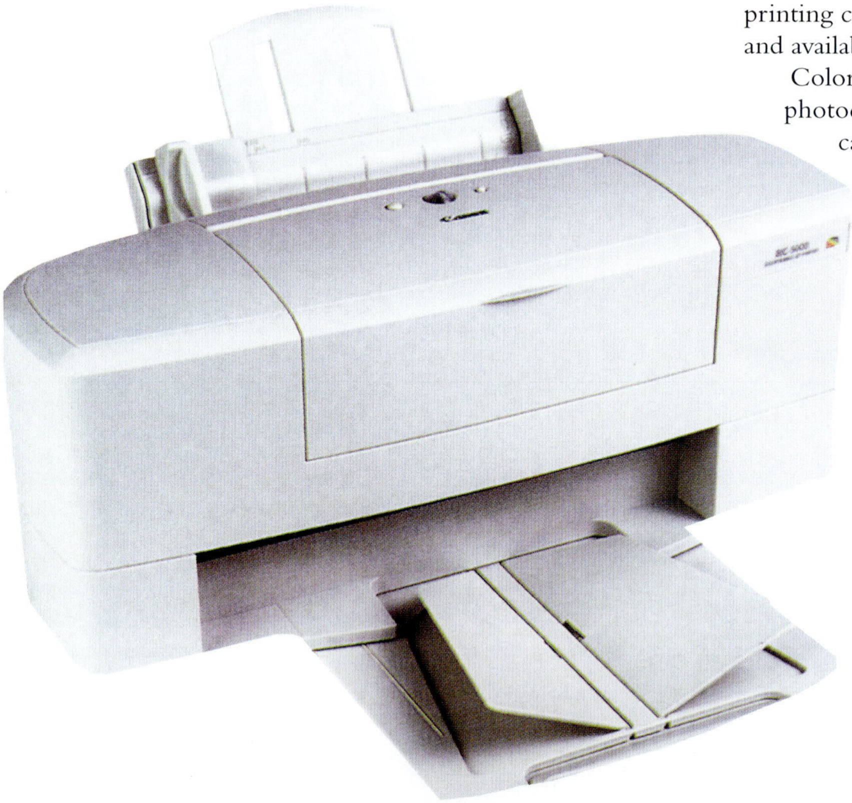

Desktop inkjet printer
This technology is nearing professional output quality at very affordable prices. Inkjet printers can print onto a range of receivers, ranging from gloss art paper to transparent film and even heavy watercolour paper.

Storage and archive

Storage of digital files during and after creation is of vital importance to the artist. The nature and size of digital image files mean that the computer's hard disk will fill up very quickly. There are a number of storage devices available at reasonable cost. Removable disks are ideal for back-up in case of computer failure, but are not reliable enough for long-term archiving.

CD writers or burners are relatively inexpensive and will copy digital data onto a compact disk, a safe and inexpensive method of saving work for long-term archiving. Technology is now available that enables a special CD to be re-written repeatedly. However, this is more expensive than standard CD technology, and does not offer any other advantages.

DEVICE	CAPACITY
Internal Hard Disk	1.0gb–12gb
External Hard Disk	4.0gb–72gb
Jaz Cartridge	2.0gb
Jaz Cartridge	1.0gb
CD	650mb
Zip Disk	250mb
Zip Disk	100mb
DVD-RAM	5.2gb
DVD	2.6gb
Floppy Disk	1.4mb
Magneto Optical (MO)	128mb–2.6gb
DAT Tape	1.3gb–70gb

Superdisk
Removable storage in the form of the Superdisk. Capable of holding 120mb of information, this is the ideal solution for short term back-up and transference of files. Superdisk drives are also compatible with standard floppy disks.

Zip drive
The industry standard for removable disks, the Zip technology can hold 100Mb or 250Mb on a disk not much bigger than a floppy. Drives are available built into some computer systems.

	PROGRAM	TYPE OF PROGRAM	PUBLISHER	WEBSITE
XRES	XRES 2.0	Image editing	Macromedia	www.macromedia.com
Photoshop	PHOTOSHOP 5.0	Image editing	Adobe	www.adobe.com
Illustrator	ILLUSTRATOR 8.0	Vector graphics		
PhotoDeluxe	PHOTODELUXE	Image Editing		
Painter	PAINTER 5.5	Real media paint package	MetaCreations	www.metacreations.com
Art Dabbler	ART DABBLER	Cut down version of Painter		
ColorIt	COLORIT 4.0	Paint package	MicroFrontier Inc.	www.microfrontier.com
CorelDRAW	CORELDRAW 8	Vector graphics	Corel	www.corel.com
CorelPAINT	CORELPHOTOPAINT 8	Image editing		
LivePIX	LIVEPIX 2.0 DELUXE	Image editing	Live Picture Inc.	www.livepicture.com
FreeHand	FREEHAND	Vector	Macromedia	www.macromedia.com

Software and plug-ins

The table opposite lists just some of the software available to the digital artist. Consider the differences between painting bitmap software, image editing bitmap software and vector-based graphics applications when buying. Vastly different results will be achieved with the different packages, so try all three types and, ideally, purchase software from each catagory. For even greater compatibility, buy software from the same producers, for example Adobe Photoshop and Illustrator.

Plug-ins

The following table of plug-ins are available on both PC and Mac and are compatible with any software that is Photoshop plug-in compatible. Check the producer's website for compatibility.

Plug-in

PROGRAM	TYPE OF PROGRAM	PUBLISHER	WEBSITE
Andromeda Series 1:	Photography filters Optical lens effects	Andromeda	www.andromeda.com
Andromeda Series 3:	Screen filter Greyscale to line art conversions		
Andromeda Shadow Filter	Shadow generation		
Andromeda VariFocus Filter	Photographic selective focus		
EdgeWizard 2	Edge blending	Chromagraphics	www.chromagraphics.com
Eye Candy 3.0	Interesting effects	Alienskin	www.alienskin.com
Xenofex	16 special effects		
Paint Alchemy 2	Paint and organic effects	Xaos Tools	www.xaostools.com
Total Xaos	Special effects bundle		
Photo/Graphic Edges 3.0 Volume I Photo/Graphic Edges 3.0 Volume II Photo/Graphic Edges 3.0 Volume III Photo/Graphic Patterns	Traditional edge effects Geometric edge effects Artistic edge effects Dynamic background patterns		
Ultimate Texture Collection Volume I Ultimate Texture Collection Volume II Ultimate Texture Collection Volume III	Paper and fabric Stone and metal Art and organics		
Typo/Graphic Edges	Type or graphics edge effects filter	Auto F/X	www.autofx.com
PhotoFrame Volume 1 PhotoFrame Volume 2	Creative edges/frames Creative edges/frames	Extensis	www.extensis.com
PhotoTools 3.0	Useful production and effects tools		
Intellihance 4.0	Visual colour correction image enhancement tool		
HVS ColorGIF 2.0	Image compression	Digifrontiers	www.digfrontiers.com
HVS Toolkit	Photoshop production tools for web designers		

Digital Tools

Importing images

Unlike the traditional artist, whose materials are portable, the digital painter cannot take a computer, monitor and tablet into the countryside to draw and paint. Reference photographs, therefore, become the basis of sketching and painting. The computer artist has several ways of importing images into paint and image manipulation software.

Scanners

Their relatively low cost and ease of use mean that desktop scanners are the first choice of image input devices. A desktop or flatbed scanner works by shining white light across a reflective or transparent photograph onto the scanner's charged couple device (CCD). This chip records the image and converts it to a digital file.

Photo CDs

Images can be scanned onto Kodak PhotoCD when you process conventional photographic film. The CD is returned with your prints and normally contains high- and low-resolution versions of your images saved as TIFFs or JPEGs. These files can be opened in Photoshop.

Video

A video grabber can be used to capture images from a normal VCR. However, images tend to be of very low quality, as videotape has a low resolution compared with other input devices.

Video camera

As with a VCR, video camera images can be captured and used as reference for painting and sketching.

Digital video camera

The digital video camera has a number of advantages over ordinary video, the main one being that the imagery has been recorded as a digital signal and so does not have to be converted or grabbed. Most digital video cameras can be connected to the computer through firewire technology.

Digital still camera

Still photographs are taken with a digital camera, with images being saved as JPEGs onto a Compact Flash or Smartmedia card.

DVD

The digital versatile disk can be read by most new computer systems.

Internet

The Internet provides a rich source of images for the artist. While they tend to be quite small and are only screen resolution, they can still be useful.

Clip art

There are thousands of CDs containing ready-made art and photography. A disk tends to be packaged according to subject matter; people, places, animals and so on. Each maker's CD will contain information on use of the images and their copyright.

Direct input

Images can be traced using a tablet and stylus. By placing a photograph onto the surface of the tablet – some have a transparent sleeve to put photos under – the artist can simply trace the image into the paint program.

COPYRIGHT

Copyright laws prevent the use or reproduction of images. Care must be taken when using any images created by another person or company. If in any doubt, it is best to ask permission or avoid using them altogether.

A typical Internet interface

The Internet is useful for researching images, although they will only usually be at screen resolution. Some images can be downloaded at full resolution using FTP software.

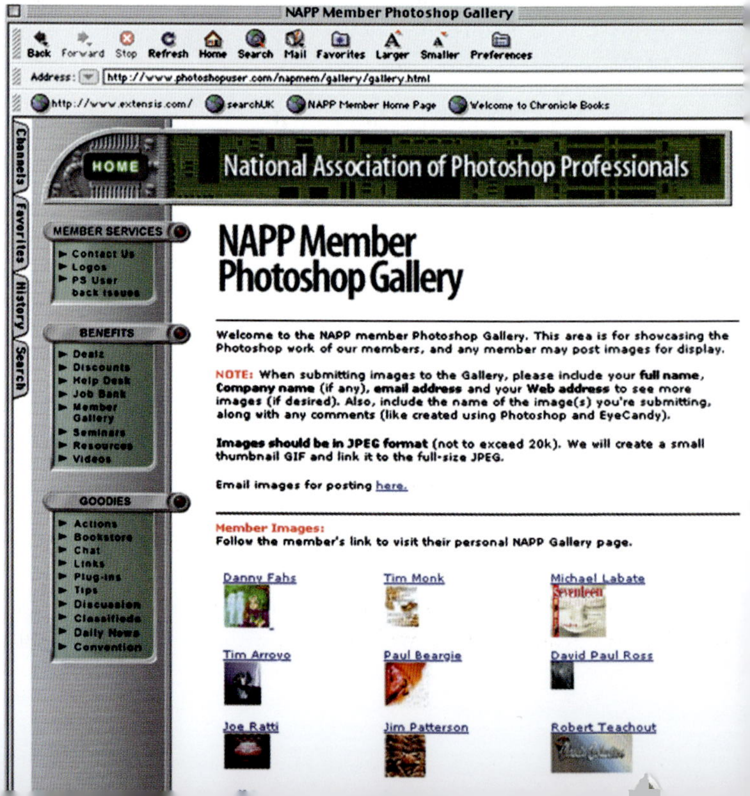

Digital Colour

To the traditional artist colour represents the building blocks of painting. It is the foundation onto which the painter builds up his work through the use of tone, light and form. For the digital artist to achieve results similar to the 'real media', time-honoured techniques, such as aerial perspective, high and low key painting and using colour to express mood, still need to be observed.

However, a whole new set of colour rules has to be learnt and applied sympathetically by the digital artist. The electronic painter must understand and anticipate the outcome of inverting a colour, shifting the hue or adjusting the brightness values on screen.

Additive and subtractive colour

It is important for the digital artist to understand how colour differs on-screen and in print, and how they complement each other. This relationship is vital when using colour tools in paint and image editing software.

Colour on screen is made up from three primary colours: red, green and blue (commonly referred to as RGB). When all three are mixed together at full strength they produce pure white light. Mixing together two additive, or screen primaries, will create a third colour that is called a subtractive primary. Red and green mixed at full strength will give yellow. Green and blue make cyan and blue and red create magenta (see Figure 1).

In the same way that two additive primaries combined produce a subtractive colour, two subtractive primaries will produce an additive primary. Cyan and yellow, for example, will create green. When all three subtractive primaries are added together they should, in theory, make pure black. However, the reality of impure printing inks means that a very dark brown is actually produced (see Figure 2).

Hue, saturation and brightness

HSB are the three variables that make up digital colour. All paint and image editing programs contain colour-mixing tools that give you control over these elements.

Hue is the name given to each colour, indicating its position in the spectrum. For example red, blue, green and so on. The traditional pigment-based colour wheel used by artists is made up of the spectrum colours arranged in order. It starts with yellow, travelling through green to blue, violet, red, orange and back to yellow (see Figure 3).

Primary hues are those colours that cannot be obtained by mixing. They are red, yellow and blue. Secondary hues are those colours mid-way between the primaries and are the result of mixing two primaries. They are green, orange and violet. Tertiary hues are found on the wheel between the primary and the secondary hues: yellow-green, blue-violet and red-orange. Artists will often limit their choice of colour

Figure 1

Figure 2

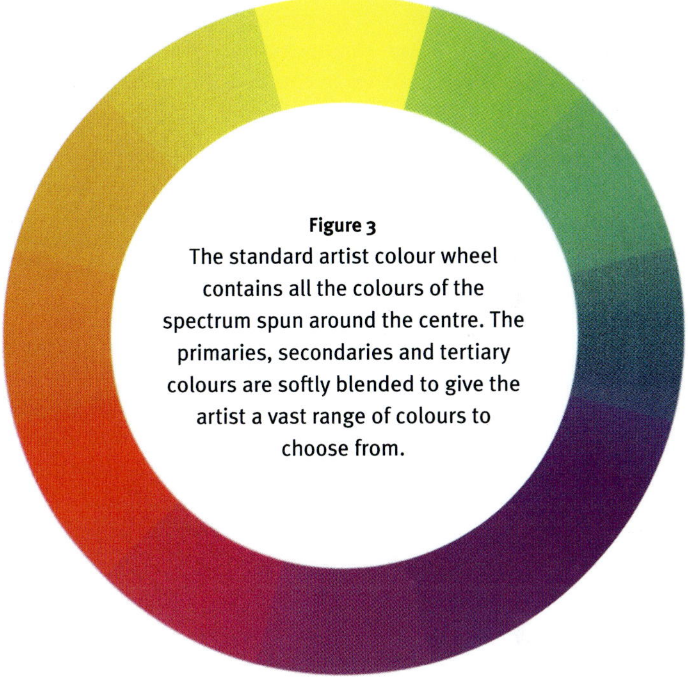

Figure 3
The standard artist colour wheel contains all the colours of the spectrum spun around the centre. The primaries, secondaries and tertiary colours are softly blended to give the artist a vast range of colours to choose from.

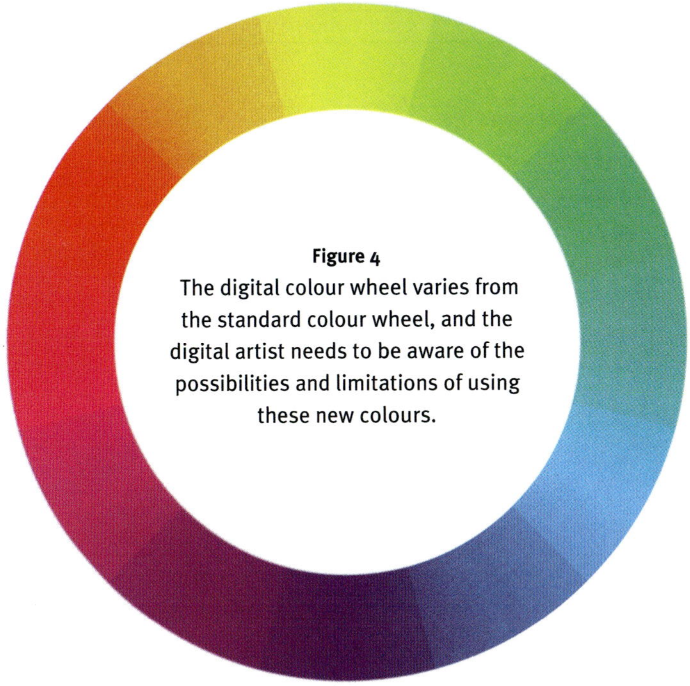

Figure 4
The digital colour wheel varies from the standard colour wheel, and the digital artist needs to be aware of the possibilities and limitations of using these new colours.

to create different moods or optical effects in their paintings.

Analogous hues are colours that are close together on the wheel, and used together they will be dominated by their common colour element. Red, red-orange and orange used in combination will give a strong fiery feel, and overall will be seen as orange.

Complementary colours sit opposite each other on the wheel, so red and green complement each other, as do blue and orange. Artists will often use a complementary colour to brighten colours or to create shadows.

Saturation is the colour's strength or purity. Saturated colours will be bright and strong, while desaturated colours will contain grey. When mixing colours in most paint programs the saturation value can be adjusted from +100%, giving the strongest values, to -100% which will result in pure grey.

Brightness is the third variable when mixing digital paints. This refers to the colour's luminance value, or its darkness or lightness. Again, the brightness value can be adjusted to +100% to give white, or -100% to give black.

The digital colour wheel

The electric artist needs an understanding of the screen-based primaries (RGB) and how they complement the print primaries (CMY). Their relationship can be represented by another colour wheel that shows the two colour modes together. Again, the colours are based around the wheel clockwise, with yellow at the top, then green, cyan, blue, magenta, red and back to yellow (see Figure 4 on page 27).

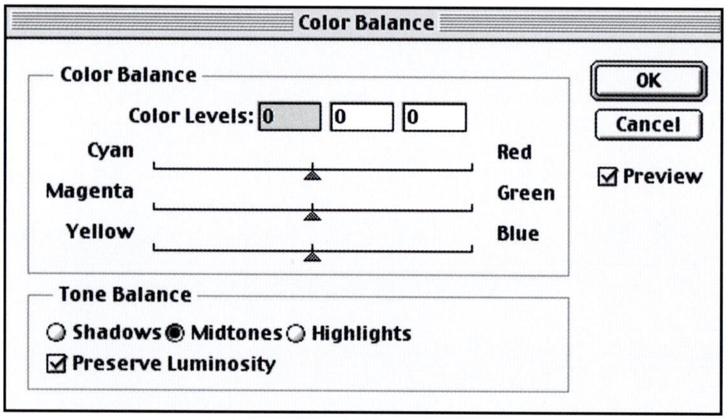

Colour Balance
The Colour Balance interface allows the user to control and adjust the three screen primaries (RGB) of the image, or a selection within the image. The effects can be limited to the shadow, mid-tone or highlight areas. When correcting an image always adjust the mid-tones first.

Inverting Colour

These two images show a technique that can only be achieved electronically. The image was first inverted giving a negative image – dark tones become light, and light dark. The colours are all shifted exactly halfway around the colour wheel. Finally, the Hue dialogue was opened and the colours were again shifted exactly halfway around the wheel. The finished image has negative tones of dark and light but has retained the original colours.

Preparing scanned images

If you are scanning images to use as a basis for your artwork, you will need to correct any defects before you begin painting. The better the quality of your scan, the better your final artwork will be. A good scan will contain the full range of tones, as well as being sharp and bright, and while most scanners will do an adequate job there is normally room for improvement. Photoshop has powerful correction tools to help you improve your scan quality; sharpness, detail, brightness, hue and saturation can all be adjusted.

Sharpening detail

Most scanners, particularly desktop scanners, tend to scan an image slightly softly. It is good practice to run the Unsharp Mask filter, once your scan is complete, to sharpen up lost detail. Unsharp mask works by increasing the contrast only on areas where there is already a strong tonal change. For example, if an image of a car was scanned and the Unsharp Mask filter applied, the edges of the doors and the outline would be sharpened but the smooth tonal transitions of the bodywork would be left soft. The Unsharp Mask filter is best run several times on a low setting. The other sharpen filters are too harsh and can lead to abnormal pixelation.

Brightness and contrast

Your reference image should contain the full range of tones, from black through to pure white. To adjust brightness and contrast use Photoshop's levels control (Image, Adjust, Levels). The histogram shows the amount of colour in the image across the range from black to white. To improve contrast, move the black and white pointers in until they meet with the edges of the histogram. This will spread the image's tonal range to its maximum, giving good dark shadows and bright highlights. Finally, adjust the grey slider to change the overall brightness of the image, moving it left to increase and right to decrease brightness.

Removing colour casts

The colour balance palette is used to remove any unwanted colour casts from the scanned image. The colour balance of the image can be adjusted by the red, green and blue components and the effects can be limited to shadow, mid-tone and highlight areas. Balance the mid-tones to correct the overall colour balance and then adjust the shadows and highlights until you are happy with the image.

Hue and saturation

Saturation can be adjusted to give richer or fuller colours, although care should be taken not to create harsh and unrealistic colours. If the image is too vibrant then it can be desaturated to remove some of the colour. The hues in the image can be rotated around the digital colour wheel and the effect can be overall or limited to parts of the colour wheel. All the reds in an image, for example, could be adjusted to make them another hue.

Descreening

Scanning from a book or magazine can lead to moiré patterns, a series of large dots caused by the printed material's screen clashing with the dot per inch of the scan. Running the despeckle filter (Filter, Noise, Despeckle) will help to reduce the pattern. Most scanners can descreen at the time of the scan.

Dust and scratches

Marks and dirt on the scanner bed will result in spots on the scan. These can be removed by painting out with a small brush, using colour from around the spot. Photoshop provides a filter (Filter, Noise, Dust & Scratches), which automatically touches out spots on the image. Marquee a small area around the spot and run the filter, which will soften the whole area and blend the surrounding colour over the spot. The filter can result in noticeable blurred areas, so run the Unsharp Mask filter after completing all spotting.

Intellihance

A completely visual way of correcting an image is to use Extensis Intellihance filter, a one-stop powerful correction tool that adjusts all possible parameters by showing you up to 25 simultaneous views of your image. You can then choose the desired effect and make further adjustments, or run the filter and let it do all the work. It can be programmed to adjust to the characteristics of your scanner.

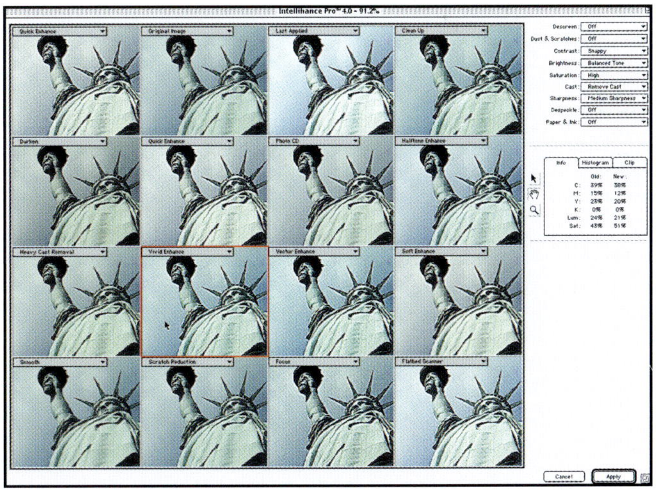

Intellihance
Very fine control over image correction is made simple.

Adjusting a scanned image

Original Scan
The original scan has poor contrast and a slightly green/yellow cast overall.

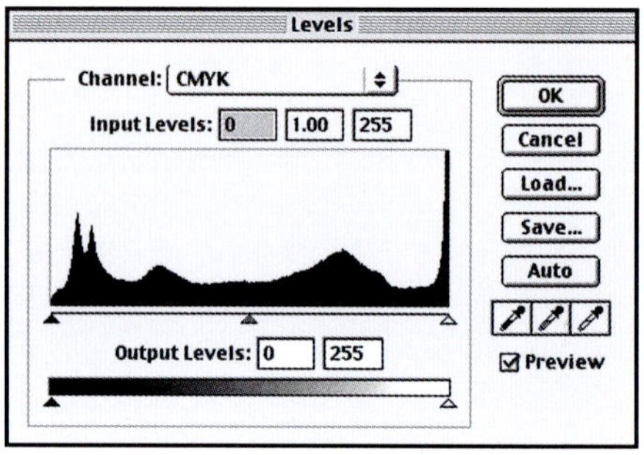

1 Levels

Adjusting the black and white input sliders distributes the image's tonal variation from pure white to black. This intensifies the image, adding more shadow and highlight detail. The grey mid-point slider adjusts the brightness of the image.

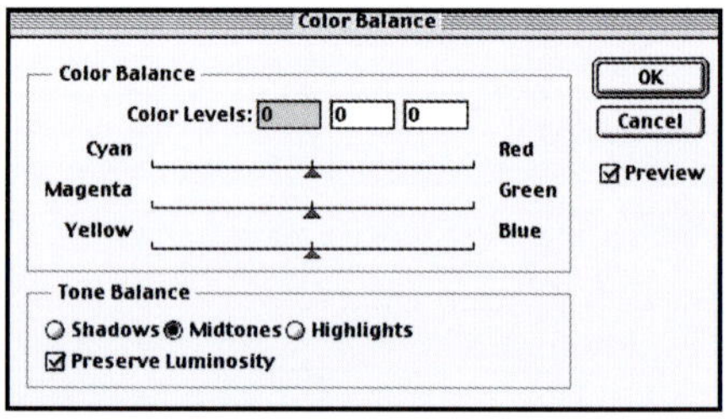

2 Colour Balance

The colour balance adjusters work by adjusting the RGB colour values in mid-tone, shadow and highlight areas. The overall colour cast was lost by adjusting the sliders.

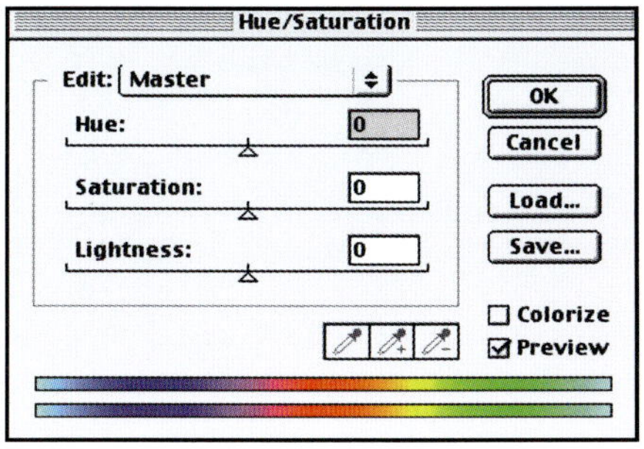

3 Saturation
To strengthen the colours, increase the saturation slightly. Care has to be taken not to strengthen the colours too much, as unrealistic colours will result.

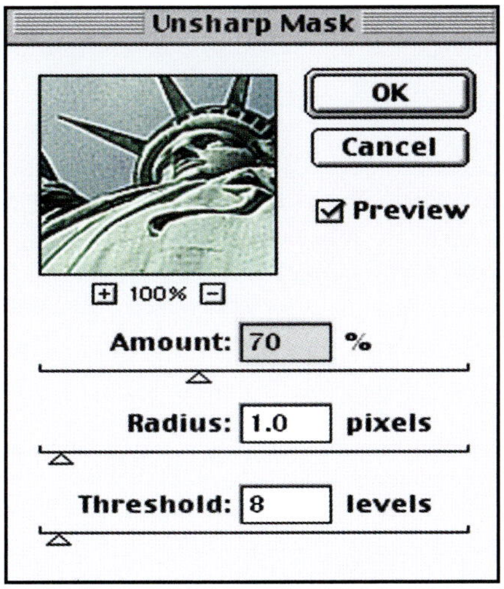

4 Unsharp Mask
The final step is to run the Unsharp Mask filter. This increases the contrast between areas where there are sharp differences between colour or tone. The effect is to retrieve some of the information lost by the scanner and other correction tools.

PROFESSIONAL SCAN QUALITY

Consider having your image produced at a professional bureau. There will be a minimal charge for this service but the quality of the scan will be far superior to that of your desktop scanner. This is a particularly useful service to utilize if the finished image will be printed on a large scale.

Scanning resolution

It is important when working with bitmap images to understand the importance of size and resolution. Bitmap images do not print well when enlarged, as the image pixels become obvious and unnatural to the eye. This is a complex subject, and what follows is only a brief explanation. However, learning the basics will help when preparing images for professional output and prevent artwork from appearing jagged.

What is resolution?

Resolution is the number of dots needed to render image detail over a given area. For output devices, such as printing, the standard unit of measurement is dots per inch (dpi), representing the number of dots printed over a linear inch. For computers and scanners the standard of measurement is pixels per inch (ppi). A pixel is the smallest unit or building block of an image.

Bit depth

Scans can contain varying amounts of information depending on the colour mode being used. Colour modes directly relate to the image's bit depth and the size of the file. The higher the bit depth the more information your scanner will have to record, and the larger the file size will be.

1-bit images

A bit is a 1 or 0, or an On or Off switch. In a 1-bit or bitmap image each pixel can only be black or white. This is the least memory intensive colour mode, as there are only two possibilities for each pixel in an image.

Greyscale

At pixel level, greyscale images are made up of 8 bits of data or 256 levels of grey, including black and white.

RGB

The most common colour mode for working in, RGB is made up of three greyscale images. One for red at 256 levels, one for blue at 256 levels and one for green at 256 levels. 24 bits of information are therefore needed.

CMYK

The four-colour printing process mode is made up of a greyscale image for all four channels—cyan, magenta, yellow and black. 32 bits of information are needed.

Screen ruling

The final piece of information needed to understand the best scanning resolution is dependent on the output device you are going to use. The screen ruling is the number of lines or rows of dots that a printer uses to produce a half tone. This is measured in lines per inch (lpi). Typical examples are newspapers at 80lpi, magazines at 133lpi and books at 150-175lpi.

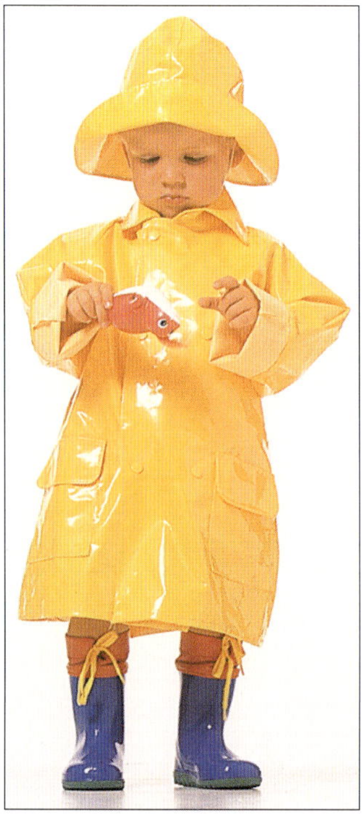

This image is 300dpi, the correct resolution for this size of picture.

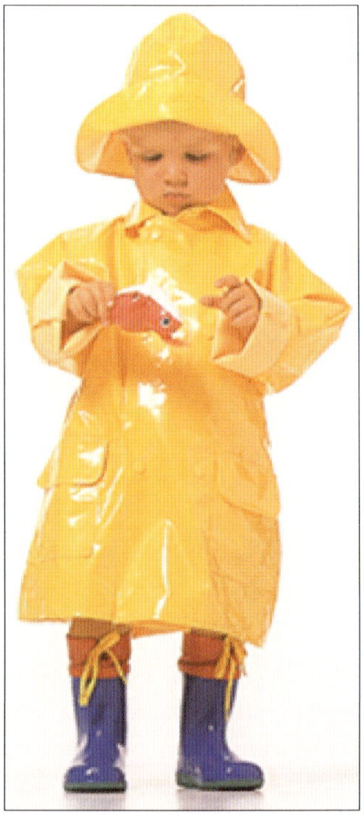

This image is 100dpi, so the picture has a jagged appearance.

Using Photoshop to decide

The simplest way to determine the size of your new artwork is to open a new file in Photoshop at the size you want to print at. Change the resolution to twice the screen ruling and read off the file size in Megabytes (Mb). When scanning, adjust the scan resolution until the file size of your scan is the same as the Photoshop file.

AT A GLANCE

To produce a scan of sufficient quality the ppi scanned should be two to three times the screen ruling of the output device. If the image being scanned needs to print with a screen ruling of 150lpi, the scan must be at 300ppi to reproduce the image same size. Scanning any more information will not improve quality but will greatly increase file size. If the image is to be enlarged, then the ppi for the scan will have to increase. An image being printed at 200%, with 150lpi screen ruling, would need to be scanned at 600ppi, or twice 300ppi.

Digital supports

The digital artist does not have to limit himself to smooth papers with no resist. There are electronic tools to recreate heavy watercolour papers, canvas and burlap. Using a texture or paper surface gives the artwork a naturalistic feel and can enhance the qualities of pencil and brushwork.

Creating textures

Scanning real papers or interesting textures is the simplest way to achieve a realistic texture on screen. Care has to be taken with brightness and contrast in order to achieve the best results.

Creating through filters

Running filters onto a flat tone or colour can create effective paper textures. The simplest technique is to run a Noise filter with a high setting and then blur it to reduce harshness. With experimentation a whole range of papers and textures can be created in this way.

Filtering

Some filters have a texture setting that will act upon the image to create the effect of paper or canvas. Adobe's Underpainting filter renders a realistic canvas texture.

Painter's surface control

MetaCreations Painter contains a surface control filter that produces realistic watercolour paper with controls over grain size and lighting direction.

Real paper

Another texturizing technique is to print out the final artwork onto a textured or watercolour paper. Most inkjet printers have settings for heavier, textured papers and experimenting with different surfaces can yield interesting results.

Apply Surface Texture
Painter's Surface Control filter (Effects, Surface Control, Apply Surface Texture) renders a paper surface onto the image. The image will react with the paper's key to give a broken colour effect. The filter gives control over paper grain and softness.

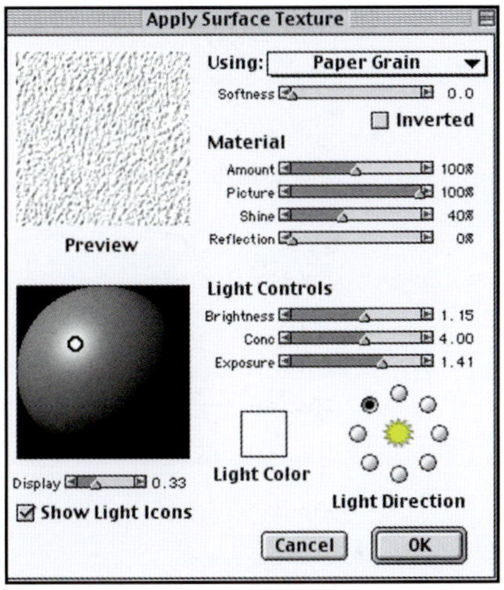

The Surface Control filter was run on this pencil portrait to produce a heavily textured watercolour paper.

TIPS

- The beauty of working with digital papers is that they can be applied to the artwork after the image has been created.
- Several copies of the artwork can be made with different paper textures.

How to use a plug-in

A plug-in is a piece of software that has been designed to plug into image editing or painting software. Generally, they are small programs that work within other programs and can be used to change the appearance of an image. Plug-ins range from image effect filters to image enhancement and colour correction tools.

Plug into your software

The plug-in software will be loaded onto the computer in the same way as any new software but will usually be placed into a folder in the mother program called plug-ins or filters. When the mother program is launched the plug-in will be available either through a pull-down menu or keystroke.

Compatibility

The standard for image processing is Photoshop compatible plug-ins. The same architecture is used for other paint and image software, so filters used in Photoshop can also be used in Painter, ColorIt, etc.

Using filters

When the filter is launched the plug-in interface will become live. There is usually a small preview window and sliders to adjust any variables available with the plug-in. Adjust to suit your requirements and press the OK button. After a short processing time you will be able to see the effects of the filter.

Plug-in brushes

The Deep Paint plug-ins include real media brushes that work directly within Photoshop. This sketch was made using several variations of large chalk brushes. Plug-in brushes give the artist greater control over parameters of brush direction and paper reaction that would be hard to replicate using filters alone.

Using brushes

Some plug-ins give you new brushes to use rather than filters. Wacom's pen tools filters give the user new tools designed for use with the Intous range of tablets. They include a pen for chiselling out in 3D, a brush that lays metal leaf onto an image, superputty (a tool that moves an image around as if it were liquid) and brush on Noise, a tool that adds grain to an image as you paint. RightHemisphere's Deep Paint plug-in works within Photoshop to recreate natural paint media. Filters and brushes are available for chalk, oil paint, watercolour and pencil, among others.

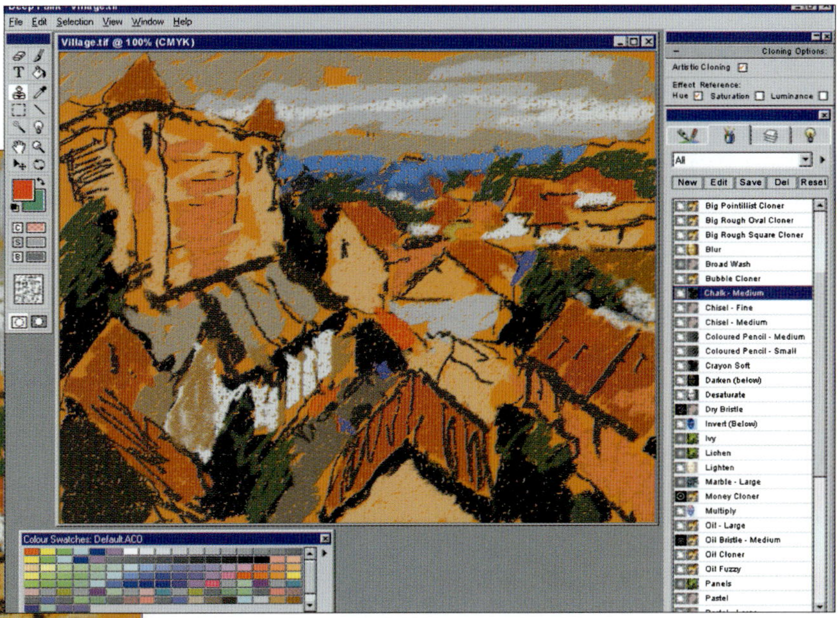

Deep Paint interface
The interface for RightHemisphere's Deep Paint plug-in is far more involved than a standard one-media filter. Effects and brushes can be accessed from the interface, giving greater control over parameters.

The two landscape images on these pages were created using brushes and filters from Deep Paint. The landscapes were rough sketches based loosely around the work of Paul Cézanne. Chalk brushes and filters were used to rapidly draw the shapes and colours.

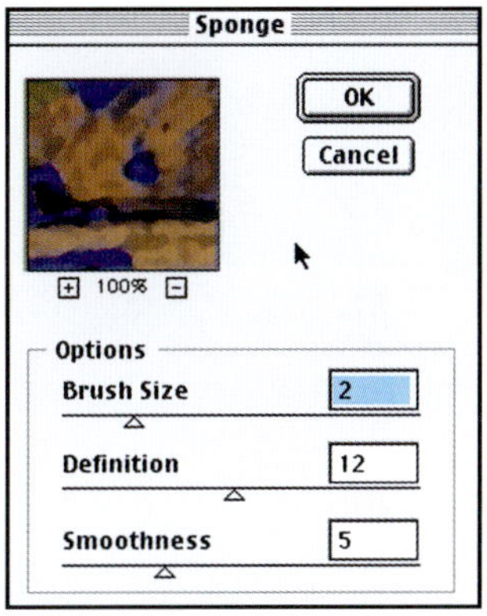

Filter interface
A typical filter interface contains a small preview window to show the effects after the filter has been run. There are usually sliders and/or numerical input fields for adjusting the filter's variables. Clicking in the preview window will show the unfiltered image. This is useful for judging how strong the filter effects are.

Tips

When a filter is updated or upgraded the effect achieved is often quite different to the previous version.

- Keep the old filter. Running the two filters independently of each other can create some interesting effects.
- If there is a software clash, with two filters having the same name, simply take one out of the program's plug-ins folder. Replace or change over when you need the other version of the filter.

Production plug-ins

There are a series of plug-ins designed to help with production, rather than image editing. These include tools for automatic colour correction, creating colour separations to CMYK or Hexachrome printing, creating file formats for web graphics and converting files for use within other applications.

Pen and ink with a tablet

Pen and ink techniques range from loose marker work to very detailed line and crosshatching drawing. Painter's pen tools can replicate pen and ink nib pens, scratchboard tools, brush and ink and marker pens. Marker work tends to be quick and is often used for illustrational purposes. Pen and ink sketches date back to the Italian Renaissance, with master artists such as Leonardo da Vinci demonstrating the delicate tonal work that can be achieved with crosshatching techniques.

TECHNIQUES

The defining quality of ink is its fluidity of line, something that can be achieved very easily with most paint software when using a tablet and stylus. The digital artist will get the same feedback through the stylus as his real media contemporary, and is able to set brush variables to allow more ink to flow when the stylus pressure is increased. Deviate from conventional techniques and try experimenting with different papers and resists, or drawing over other media, all of which can yield interesting results.

Nib pens
The nib of the ink pen can be adjusted to suit the work being created. Variations include thick and thin nibs, calligraphic and size or weight. These can vary according to pressure on the stylus or can be fixed.

Leaky pen
MetaCreations Painter contains a pen that gives the effect of leaking ink. The faster you move the stylus the more leaks out. Careful and sparing use of this can create very realistic effects.

Resist techniques
Using a mask limits the ink to defined areas in the drawing. This technique is similar to using a rubber solution to prevent ink penetrating areas of the paper. A flower was masked out and ink brushed over the image.

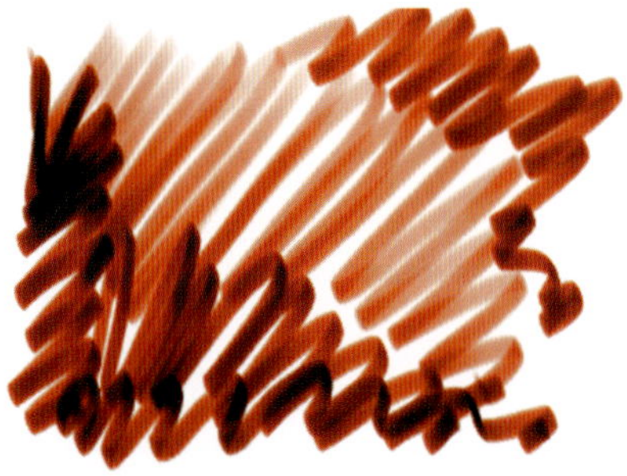

Dirty marker pens
The technique shows scribbling with a marker that is running out of ink – the more pressure applied to the stylus the darker ink. Felt-tip pens dramatically increase in depth as marks are overlaid.

Crosshatching
Pattern-making techniques work extremely well with fine felt-tip pens. Areas of tone can be built up by using several different colours.

Water and felt-tip pen
Felt-tip pen marks can be softened and smudged with a wet brush. This technique is suited to blending colours together.

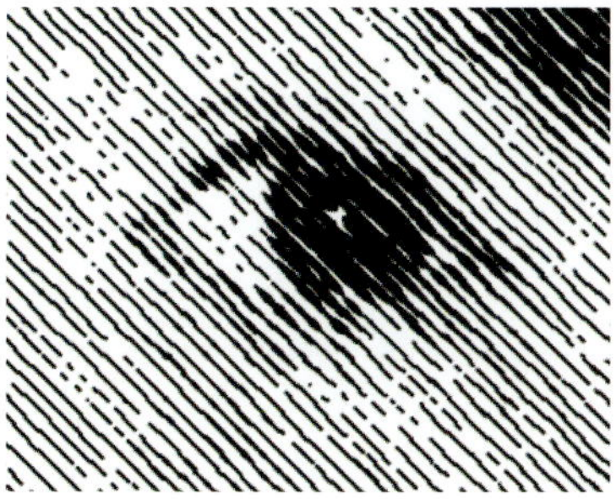

Half-tone work
The eye was drawn using a fine ink pen, using denser strokes where darker areas were needed. There are many filters that can create this effect faster and more accurately than drawing by hand.

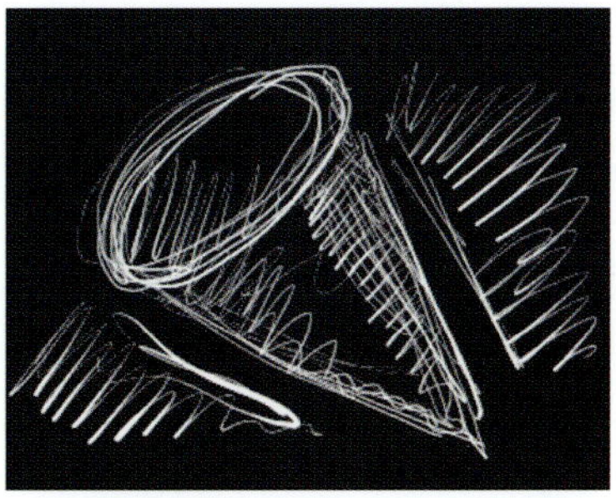

Scratchboard
This drawing was scratched out of a black base. Colour can be washed over with a watercolour brush.

SHADOW AREAS
The shadows were painted in using Illustrator's brush and pencil tools, before opening the image in Painter and softening the shadow edges with soft watercolour brushes.

The sketches for the camera and this corkscrew began in Adobe Illustrator 8. The black outlines were roughly drawn using a stylus and then adjusted to smooth out any kinks. Brushes were created for the black line work to copy the appearance of working with a paintbrush and Indian ink. Areas of colour were drawn using Illustrator's pencil tool. The images were then opened in Photoshop, some colour desaturated, and the files saved in TIFF format for printing.

Indian Ink Portrait

This portrait was drawn from a scan of an old photograph. An ink outline was very quickly roughed in using the dirty marker pen from Painter's cloner tools. Further detail was added, using black ink and a nib pen. To add more tones, a wet paintbrush smudged some of the black to give a watercolour effect. The resulting image is very similar to real media Indian ink and wash drawings.

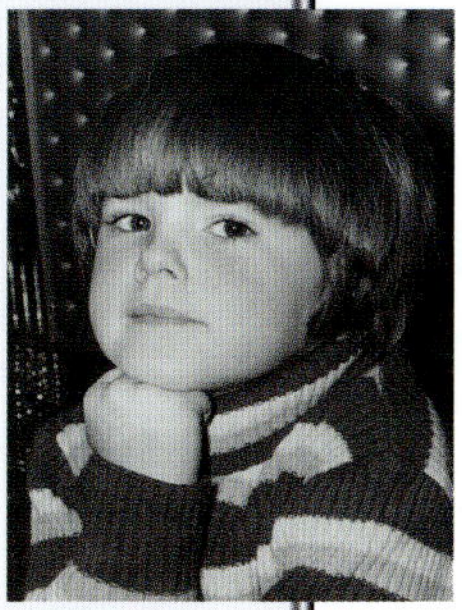

HEAVY CALLIGRAPHIC LINE WORK
The line work was drawn in Adobe Illustrator, before applying the calligraphy styling to the brush. The smooth lines are very similar to the flowing brushwork that a soft sable brush and Indian ink would give.

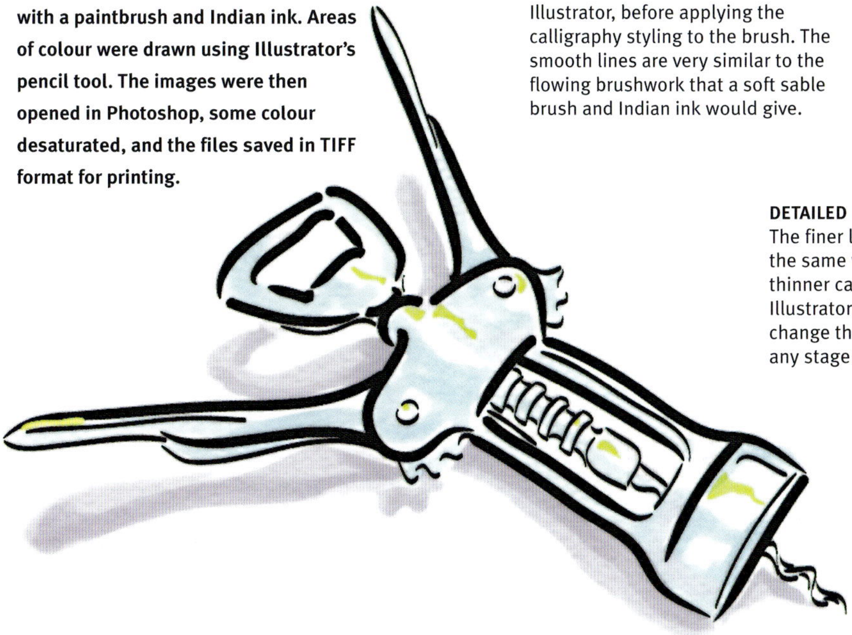

DETAILED LINES
The finer lines were created in the same way but resized to a thinner calligraphy brush. Illustrator allows the user to change the weight of the line at any stage in the drawing.

Tips

- Always set the brush tracking preferences before ink work. It is important that the computer can keep up with the fast movements of the stylus.
- To give black ink work a slightly transparent appearance try running a painting filter on your finished drawing.

Pen and ink plug-ins

Loose pen and ink techniques are difficult to recreate with a plug-in. This medium lends itself to expressive work through dramatic pen strokes and capturing this feel is best not attempted with plug-in filters. However, detailed studies of line and tone through crosshatching techniques work very well with filters.

To achieve the best possible results it is important to start with an original image that contains a full range of tones. Adjusting the levels to give pure highlights and rich blacks will allow the filter to lay detailed tonal areas, with solid shadows and transparent whites. As the filter tends to darken the image, it is good working practice to increase the brightness once the image is complete. This also burns out highlight areas.

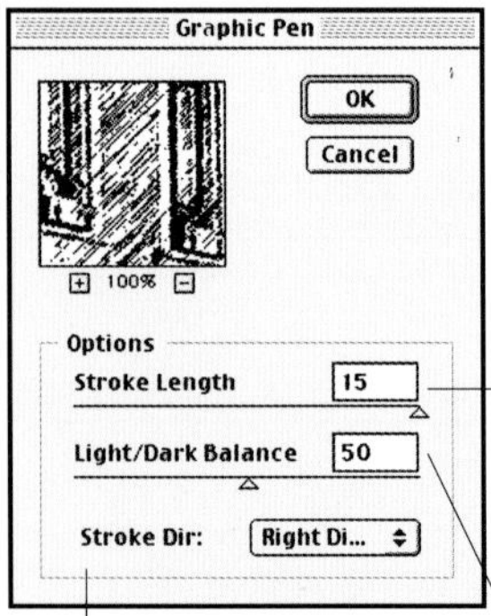

Graphic Pen Interface/Variables

Options

STROKE LENGTH
1–15 (the maximum distance in pixels of a pen stroke)

LIGHT/DARK
Balance 0–100 (Below 50% the image gets darker overall and above 50% the image is lightened)

STROKE DIRECTION
(The direction of the pen marks)
Right or Left diagonal
Vertical
Horizontal

Options Stroke Length **15**
Light/Dark Balance **50%**
Stroke Direction
Right Diagonal

Options Stroke Length **15**
Light/Dark Balance **30%**
Stroke Direction
Vertical

Options Stroke Length **5**
Light/Dark Balance **75%**
Stroke Direction
Left Diagonal

Options Stroke Length **8**
Light/Dark Balance **10%**
Stroke Direction
Left Diagonal

Paint Alchemy Ink Marks

Xaos Tools' Paint Alchemy was run on this image to replicate shorter pen marks. A coloured paper was used as a base, adding an interesting tonal effect.

Inklination

The Inklination Crosshatching filter provides incredible control over crosshatching techniques. Variables include stroke thickness, nib size, roughness, line length and amplitude, and how steady the lines are. Given all these variables, the digital pen becomes a powerful and fully adjustable drawing tool.

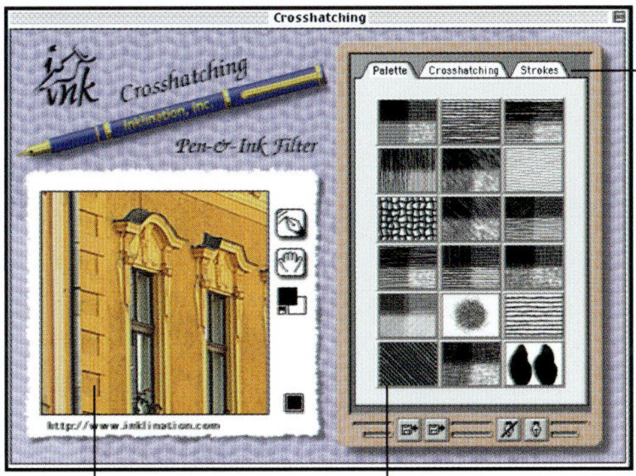

TABBED MENUS
Clicking on the tabs brings forward the interfaces for more precise control over the pen's variables. Nib size, line length and steadiness are variable either by sliders or numerical inputs.

PREVIEW
The filter has a large preview area that shows precisely the effects the filter will have on the image.

SWATCHES
The preset swatches show some of the effects possible. They are selected by clicking on the desired swatch.

Tips

The computer's line work is very exacting and can easily look too precise. Follow these directions to give your work a hand-drawn real media quality.

1 Establish the outlines of your image by running the Find Edges or Trace Contour filters.

2 When you are happy with the basic line work run the Gaussian blur filter to soften lines, being careful not to lose all detail.

3 Using the controls for contrast and brightness, adjust contrast to a high setting to re-establish rich black tones.

4 Adjust the brightness control to make the line weight increase or decrease, giving a far more natural feel to the line work.

The ink work on this circular saw was achieved by running non-ink filters. The image's contrast was greatly increased, while background detail was painted away using a large brush and opaque white colour. Two copies of the image were created: the Find Edges filter was run on one, and the Poster Edges filter on the other. Both were converted to greyscale and the line work softened with a slight Blur filter. The contrast was then adjusted to retrieve the dark tones. Finally, the two images were combined and a soft background airbrushed in.

X RES
Photoshop
Illustrator
PhotoDeluxe
Painter
Art Dabbler
Drawing Tablet

Pencil with a tablet

The pencil is the most basic drawing tool used by artists today. The digital sketcher has access to every weight and size of pencil and has the advantage that they'll never need sharpening. This is one of the most versatile of digital tools and, with a little thought and practice, incredibly realistic pencil drawings can be created.

THE TABLET

The stylus is the ideal tool for creating pencil drawings. Pressure sensitivity can be set so that line weight, tone and the pencil's reaction to the surface of the paper are all controllable. Most styli have an eraser, which is used by turning the pen upside down.

TECHNIQUES

These techniques were created in MetaCreations Painter. Similar effects can be achieved in other programs by drawing with a small brush and then running pencil filters on sections. This is a more time consuming technique but yields realistic pencil work.

Line weight
Increasing pressure and speed darkens the tone. Painter's 2B pencil was used here.

Graduations
Using a soft pencil and varying the pressure allows the artist to create soft graduated effects, ideal for smooth transitions in tonal drawings.

Paper key
Drawing with soft pencil over a heavy paper. The pencil reacts with the paper's grain and, again, the use of light pressure will allow the paper to show through.

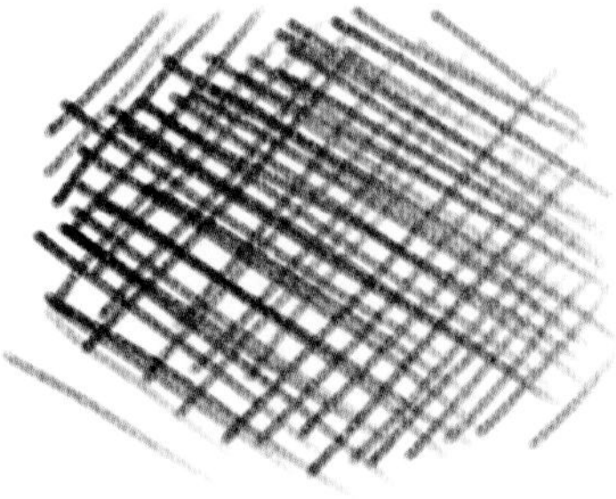

Crosshatching
A technique for producing different tonal elements utilizing fine pencil lines drawn at opposing angles. The denser the lines, the darker the optical tone.

This tonal study of a Corvette uses soft pencil strokes to build up shape and form. Detail was kept to a minimum and the tonal range was limited to keep the drawing light.

This girl's face was drawn with a range of pencil marks. A heavier weight of pencil and darker tones were used to create a dramatic atmosphere and over-emphasize the fall of light on her face.

This photograph was used as reference for the study below. The tree was kept dark, with limited highlights, while the sky was built up with crosshatching. Very subtle tonal changes are possible with this technique.

Eraser
The eraser works in the same way as its real equivalent and is accessed by turning the stylus upside down. It can be used to draw light objects out of dark backgrounds.

Smudging
The effect of smudging soft pencil work with a finger can be simulated by using a wet paintbrush loaded with no colour.

Different pencils
A range of pencil effects can be created giving different weights of line, depending on the softness and size of the lead.

Wet over pencil
Loading a watercolour brush with a light grey colour and painting over your pencil sketch gives a range of subtle tonal shifts.

X RES

Photoshop

Illustrator

PhotoDeluxe

Painter

Art Dabbler

Drawing Tablet

Coloured pencil with a tablet

Coloured pencil techniques are very similar to graphite pencil techniques. The sketcher has more flexibility, as work not only has to represent light and tone but the hue of the subject matter. Tones can be used to express aerial perspective, while complementaries can show shadow detail, and colour can express mood.

THE TABLET

The stylus as a coloured pencil allows the sketcher to work as he would normally. Fast and dynamic pencil strokes are far easier than with a mouse and the feel of holding a pencil is more natural. The stylus pressure can change line weight, tone, paper key and colour. When drawing with only two colours, the stylus can be programmed to change between the colours by increasing the pressure. Turning the stylus upside down gives access to a third colour without having to select with a mouse click.

TECHNIQUES

Our techniques were created in MetaCreations Painter. The pencil work is very realistic and easy to achieve. Other paint programs can be made to simulate pencil by drawing with small paintbrushes and then treating the work with a coloured pencil filter.

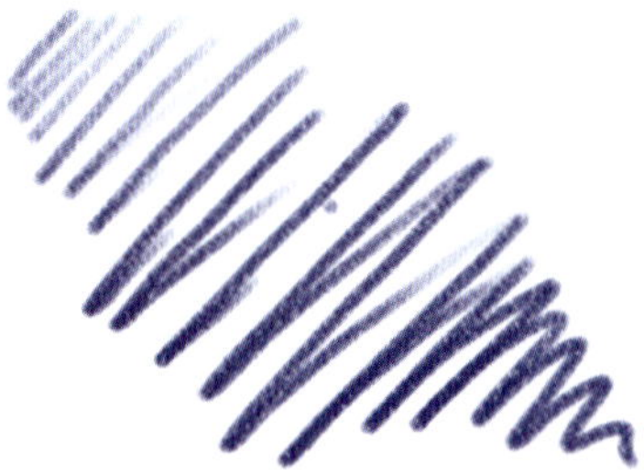

Line weight
Increasing pressure and speed darkens the tone. Colour can also change with added pressure.

Graduations
Increasing pressure smoothly over an area produces soft graduations.

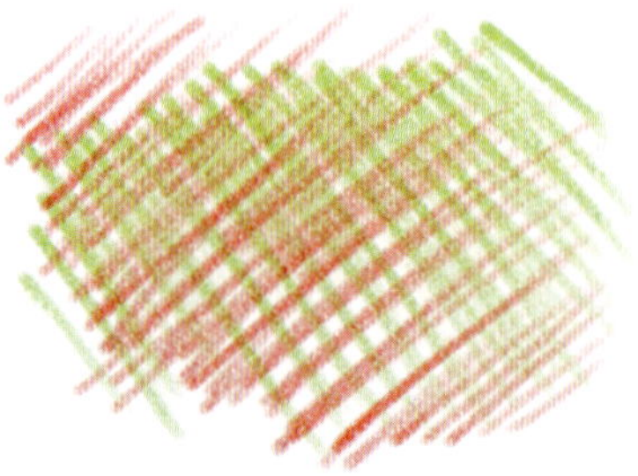

Optical mixing
By hatching one colour over a second shade the artist leaves the viewer to blend the two together. This trick is used by many artists and gives the work a light feel. Detail can be added to portraits, for example, without the work becoming too dark or heavy.

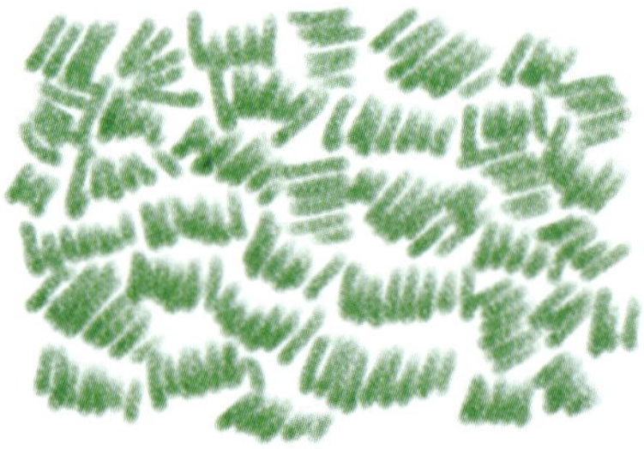

Pattern making
Using short strokes and making small patterns, textures can be built-up in the image.

Smudging
By using the eraser end of the stylus the pencil work can be smudged for very soft tonal drawing.

Bleaching
Marks can be made over flat tones using a paintbrush with white paint and a low opacity or an eraser.

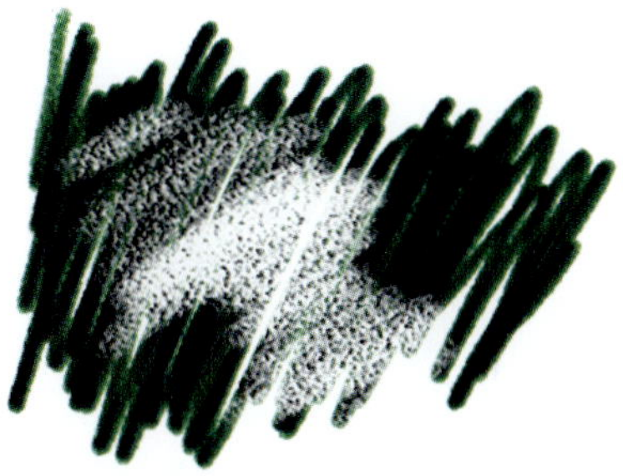

Chalk
Use white chalk over pencil work to create textured highlight areas.

Water
Using a watercolour brush over coloured pencil marks softens the line work and allows the painter to smudge colours into one another.

Emphasizing form

This coloured pencil sketch of the vase began with a scanned image that was cleaned up and colour corrected. Using this as a template, the form of the vase was sketched in using graphite pencil. Once the tonal qualities were captured the image was saved. With the new pencil sketch open, the original, corrected version was dragged onto a new layer. The image was then blended with the grey sketch and the Blending mode was changed to colour; this applies only the colour values of original onto the underlying sketch. Further tonal work was done with Photoshop's Dodge and Burn tools.

EYES
The eyes are the focal point of this portrait. Precise pencil work was used to capture subtle nuances in colour and light.

HAIR
The hair was roughly blocked in to show the changes in light. Form was emphasized by using directional lines. Finally, a few stray hairs were lightly drawn in.

LIP LINE
The lips were initially roughed in. The edges and tonal variations were carefully added.

T-SHIRT
Soft pencil work was used to lay down colour and tone. Keeping this area soft avoids taking the viewer's eyes from the face.

The graphite pencil study has been worked here with coloured pencils. The hi-key image was kept soft and bright with detail held to a minimum. Delicate work around the eyes brought the portrait to life.

Tips

An easy way to choose the colours for an image is to sample them from another image.

- Scan an image containing the colours that you want to use and sample them with the eye dropper tool.
- To simplify colour selection even further, sample from an image with a similar subject matter.

Pencil plug-ins

The digital sketcher must practice their skills in order to achieve the same qualities as real pencil, without a rigid computer structure or pattern emerging. One of the best plug-ins for pencil work is Xaos Tools' Paint Alchemy. It is very versatile and allows the user a great deal of control over variables such as brush size, colour, brush direction and angle, the brightness of the finished drawing and its transparency or the amount of white paper left empty.

Xaos Tools' Paint Alchemy filter was run on three copies of this sketch, preset at Soft Pencil Light, Soft Pencil Dark and Coloured Pencil. The copies were layered in Photoshop and, using layer masks, parts from all three images were merged together using a soft brush. The final step was to add in detail around the eyes and mouth by cloning from the original image with the stamp tool.

Paint Alchemy Interface/ Variables

BRUSH
Variations: Brush shape, Density, Position Vertical and Horizontal. All are variable to +100%. Random variation possible.

COLOUR
Variations: Brush colour, Background colour, HSB Hue Saturation, and Brightness.

SIZE
Variable by the image colour, HSB, position, or random.

ANGLE
Variable by the image colour, HSB, position, or random.

TRANSPARENCY
Variable by the image colour, HSB, position, or random.

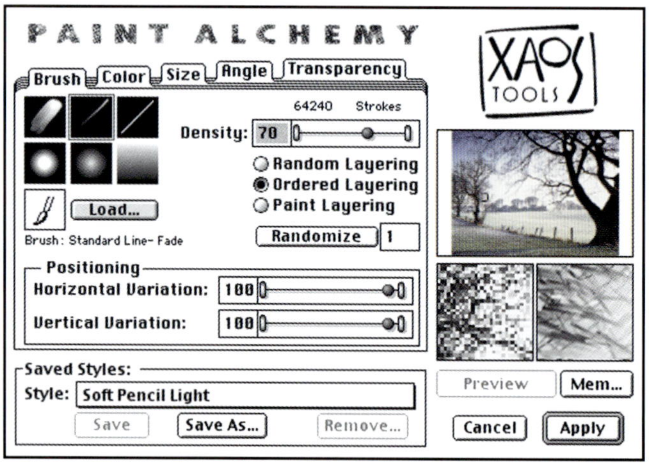

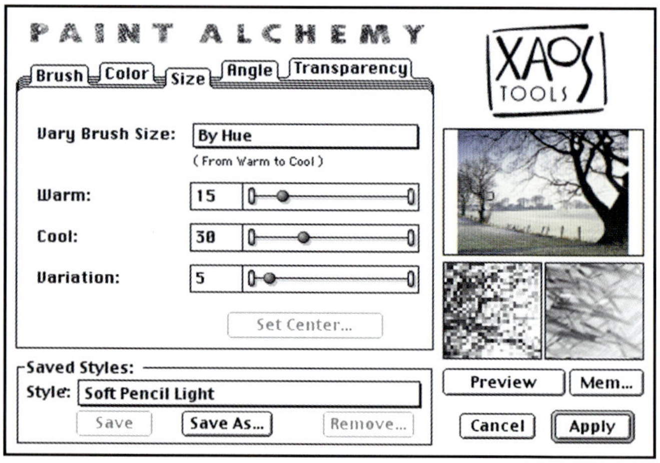

A dull winter landscape photograph was colour corrected. The image was lightened as the pencil detail tends to darken the finished image. (See page 29 Preparing Scanned Images.)

Photoshop's Find Edges filter (Filter, Stylize, Find Edges) was run to give a black and white outline.

Xaos Tools' Paint Alchemy run on default Soft Pencils Light. Variables: Colour changed from Image to Solid. A neutral graphite pencil colour was chosen.

Paint Alchemy soft pencils was then run on the above image. Variable: Colour set to From Image; stroke angle set to Brightness; transparency set to Brightness.

Default Soft Pencils Light. Variables: Colour set to From Image; stroke direction set to Brightness.

The final image combined the images above and left. The blend mode was changed to Multiply, darkening the colour sketch to give a convincing landscape study in graphite and coloured pencil.

For this sketch the filter was run as above. The brush colour was changed to white and the paper colour to a dark grey. The result was a sketch made with a white pencil onto raven paper.

Tips

- Running the same filter with different variables dramatically changes the outcome.
- Run out several versions of the same image and then combine them. The final artwork will have a greater tonal range and the pencil strokes will vary in direction and weight. This closer replicates the real media artist sketching outdoors.

X RES

Photoshop

Illustrator

PhotoDeluxe

Painter

Art Dabbler

Drawing Tablet

Charcoal with a tablet

As a drawing medium charcoal is very versatile, a quality that artists have utilized across the centuries. Its unique properties allow for a range of techniques including heavy and soft line work, soft tonal work using the side of a stick of charcoal and blending and smudging with fingers or water.

THE TABLET

Digital charcoals yield convincing line and tone work easily and swiftly. The digital tool will react with papers and other drawing media in the same way as real charcoal.

TECHNIQUES

Charcoal techniques are easily obtained with digital tools. However, achieving the spontaneity of charcoal takes practice and an understanding of real media techniques. Set as many of the pressure sensitive variables as possible and the line and tonal work will look more convincing – real charcoal never quite makes the same mark twice. Using a heavily keyed texture as a base will also improve the finished work.

Line weight
The tone varies according to the pressure and speed at which the stylus is used. Greater pressure gives darker tones. This technique is ideal for sketching areas of shade.

Sharp tip crosshatching
By using a small brush you can copy the effect of sharpened charcoal. This lends itself to creating textures through crosshatching or stippling.

Soft tone
Limiting the tool's tonal range and using a larger sized brush copies the effects gained from the side of a piece of charcoal. This is most effective for soft tonal work.

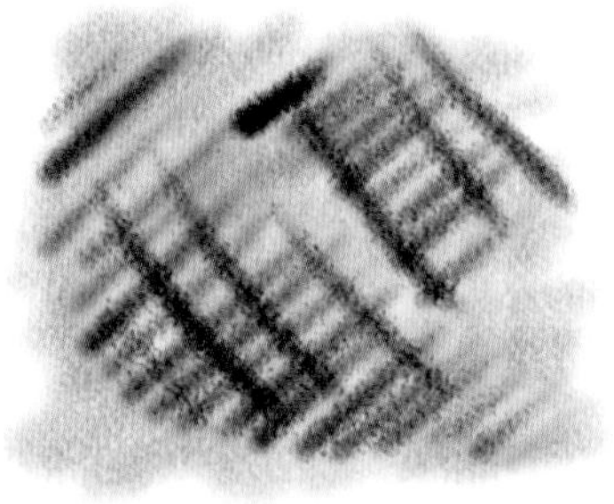

Pattern over tone
Create extra interest by using a heavier charcoal stick and hatching or scoring over a soft area.

TIPS

- Roughly lay areas of tone first and then build up detail.
- Detail can be added to a drawing by erasing areas of the image, as well as by drawing in darker areas. Try the eraser tools, or simply pick a lighter colour and draw out the highlights.
- Try the same artwork with different paper textures. Startling results appear when using an unusual texture as your base.
- Charcoal work drawn over a colour image gives the artist new possibilities to explore.

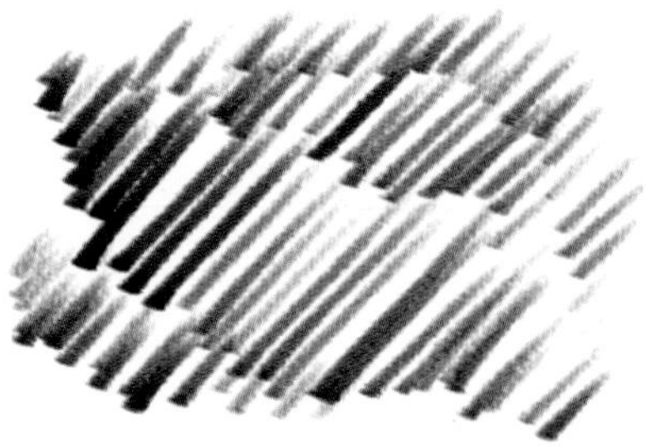

Broken charcoal
Use a square or calligraphic brush to draw, then run a Charcoal filter over small sections of your work. This will look similar to using a charcoal stick that has been snapped in two.

Smudging
Smudging charcoal is a commonly used real media technique. This can be copied by running Gaussian and Motion blurs at low settings over your drawing.

White chalk
Charcoal artists will often use white chalk over their work to add highlights. To copy this, draw the highlight areas with the same charcoal techniques but select white paint instead of black.

Heavy rough charcoal
For areas of dramatic lighting use strong random strokes, allowing the paper to show through in some lighter areas.

This portrait, drawn very rapidly from life, uses a range of techniques to create interesting textures. Detail was kept to a minimum, as the finished piece is a sketch for a more formal portrait (see page 65). The paper's key is allowed to show through, while smudging techniques give the work a convincing charcoal look.

This study of a flower was worked from a photograph, using an off-white cartridge paper scan as a digital background. The charcoal work was merged with the paper to allow the grain to show. White chalk highlights were painted in to increase the drawing's tonal range.

Charcoal plug-ins

Adobe's sketch filters Charcoal and Chalk & Charcoal filters are powerful tools in the hands of the digital painter. Fast and very easy to use, they yield impressive results with little work. Working over the image and adding a heavy paper texture will help the artist to achieve a wide range of realistic charcoal effects.

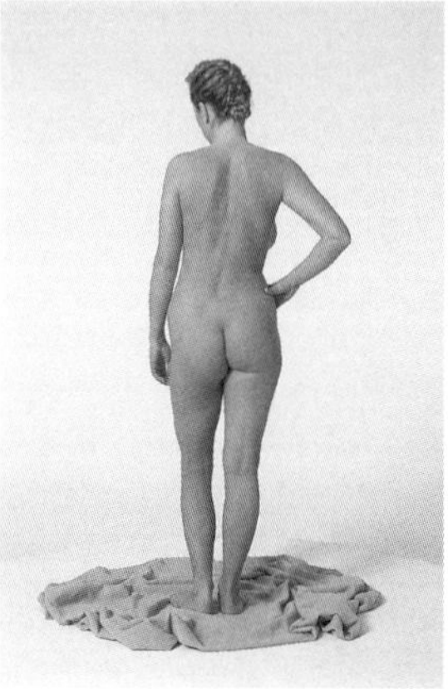

This classic image of a nude was scanned for these charcoal studies. The image was cleaned up and the brightness and contrast adjusted to lighten the image and give a greater range of tones.

Charcoal Interface/ Variables

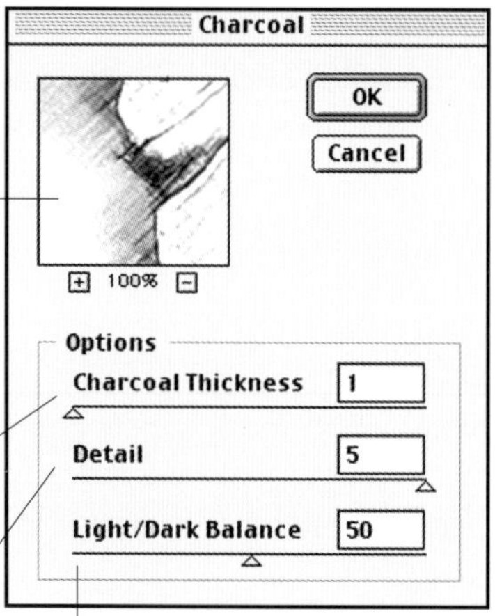

PREVIEW
The preview window is variable from 25% to 1600%. Click and hold on the preview to see the original before the filter is run

Options

CHARCOAL THICKNESS
Variable from 1–7

DETAIL
0–5

LIGHT/DARK BALANCE
0–100
(Below 50 lightens image, above 50 darkens)

Options Charcoal Thickness **1**
Detail **5**
Light/Dark Balance **50**

Options Charcoal Thickness **5**
Detail **3**
Light/Dark Balance **90**

Options Charcoal Thickness **4**
Detail **0**
Light/Dark Balance **100**

Options Charcoal Thickness **7**
Detail **2**
Light/Dark Balance **70**

Chalk & Charcoal Interface/Variables

PREVIEW
The preview window is variable from 25% to 1600%. Click and hold on the preview to see the original before the filter is run

Options

CHARCOAL AREA
Variable from 0–20

CHALK AREA
0–20

STROKE PRESSURE
0–5

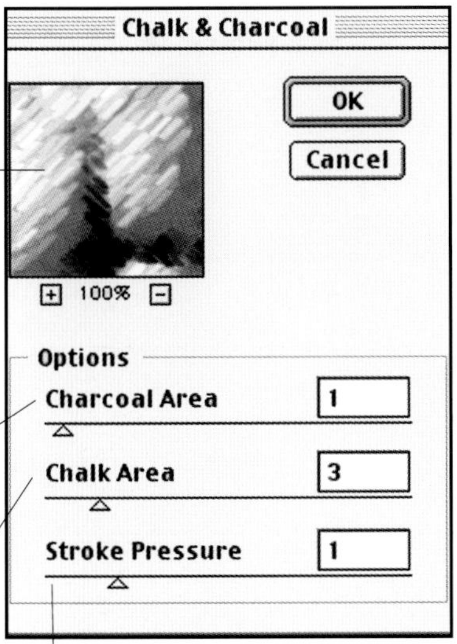

Options Charcoal Area **6**
Chalk Area **6**
Stroke Pressure **1**

Options Charcoal Area **3**
Chalk Area **5**
Stroke Pressure **1**

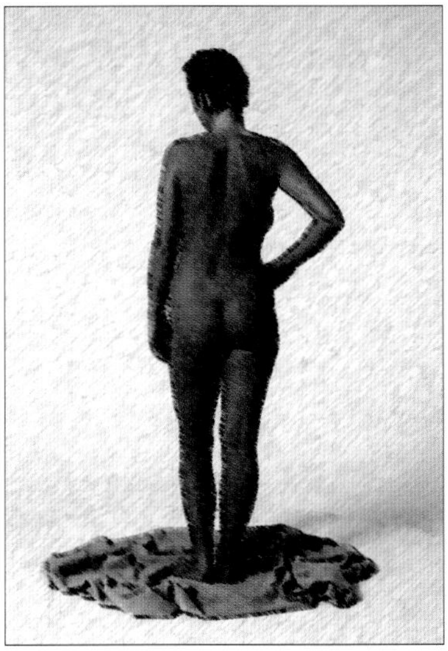

Options Charcoal Area **1**
Chalk Area **20**
Stroke Pressure **1**

Options Charcoal Area **1**
Chalk Area **3**
Stroke Pressure **1**

TIPS

- The charcoal filters tend to lose detail in the image and generally soften light edges.
- To hold detail run a pencil filter or the Photocopy filter and blend this into the charcoal image.

The final image was produced by running both the Charcoal and the Chalk & Charcoal filters. A canvas texture was added and a soft border painted in white. The image was then blended with a copy of the original image, which had been blurred heavily.

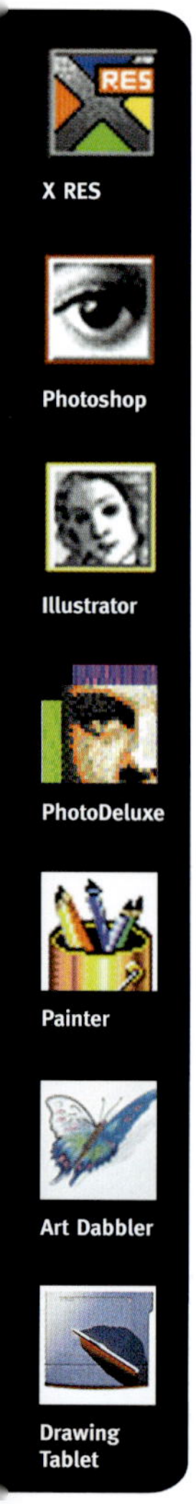

Rough pastel with a tablet

The artist can quickly and accurately render the properties of real pastels using a tablet. Areas of colour can be laid down rapidly, detail can be rendered with crosshatching, and optical mixing techniques can be employed using multidirectional strokes in a range of colours.

Experimentation with papers and textures will lead the digital artist to discover their own ways of using rough pastel. How the colour reacts with the surface texture will depend on the stylus settings and the pressure applied when drawing. Try to keep the drawing loose and free, as this medium lends itself to very expressive drawing.

Rough pastels are used by many painters when sketching out a new project. Areas of colour and tone can be laid down quickly, giving a highly textured rough image.

This image of a French street scene, painted in the style of Dufy, demonstrates how suitable the digital pastel is for rapidly creating a working sketch. It was simple to adjust the image's tonal values, while retaining vibrancy of colour.

TECHNIQUES

The following techniques are a few of the possibilities using a stylus and range of rough pastel brushes.

Laying flat tone
By maintaining equal pressure a flat tonal area can be put down. The paper's key should react with the pastel in lighter areas.

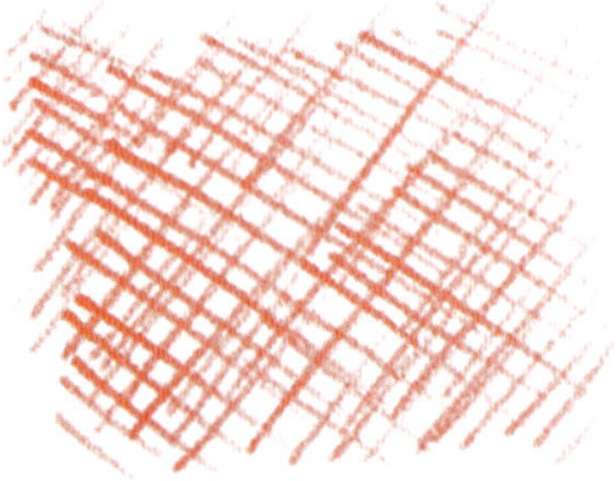

Crosshatching
Digital pastels can be sharpened to a fine point and, of course, they will not blunt. Fine crosshatching and pattern making builds up areas of tone, while retaining paper colour.

Short colour strokes
You can build areas of tone and colour by making short strokes with the pastel. Mix two or three colours together and allow the viewer's eye to blend them together.

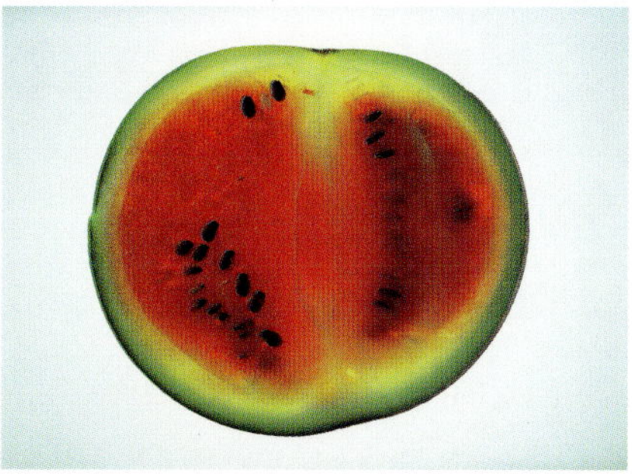

The scan, above, of a melon slice was cleaned up using the Intellihance plug-in, with settings to give a rich and saturated image. This was cloned in MetaCreations Painter (employing a technique of copying the image onto a virtual tracing paper) and traced using the Pastel Cloner brush. Brush strokes were kept short and multidirectional. The final image was again treated to brighten and saturate the colours.

Smudging
A liquid brush gives the effect of smudging pastels with a finger. A faint trace of the colour should be smudged onto the paper.

Using water to smudge
By using a watercolour brush with no colour the pastel marks can be smudged more dramatically than with the Smudging technique.

Gradations
This technique grades colour through the application of more pressure to the stylus to increase the pastel's density and colour.

Scraping away
Lay a flat tone with your pastels and then switch to the scratchboard rake tool. Use white paint to achieve the effect of scratching with a knife. This is a useful technique for placing detail back into highlights of a portrait.

Varying the pressure
By varying the pressure on the pastel the chalk will react to the paper's surface in different ways. Apply light pressure to achieve broken colour. Heavy pressure gives a solid colour with no show-through.

TIPS

Pastels are an ideal medium for roughing-out areas of colour and tone to use as a base for a more detailed study in oil paint.

- Use the scanned image as a template and draw directly on top, sampling colours from the image as you work.
- Quickly fill areas of colour, light and shade, leaving any detail until the whole image is blocked in.
- More detailed work can then be overpainted and the paint can be made to react with the original pastel sketch.

Rough pastel plug-in

Real media rough pastels are used for quickly sketching tone, colour and composition. They react to the paper's key – light pressure allowing the paper to show through and stronger pressure building up the chalk to become solid colour with no show-through.

The strength of real pastel work is in the expression of colour. The artist can alter the feel or mood of the image by simplifying the colour palette or making the colours striking and dramatic. Alter the original image's colour balance or saturation before running the Rough Pastel plug-in. To increase drama in the image adjust the saturation controls until you have vivid, bold colours.

Options Stroke Length **10**, Stroke Detail **4**, Texture **Canvas**, Scaling **75%**, Relief **20**, Lighting Direction **Top left**

Options Stroke Length **20**, Stroke Detail **10**, Texture **Burlap**, Scaling **100%**, Relief **30**, Lighting Direction **Top right**, **Inverted**

Options Stroke Length **30**, Stroke Detail **1**, Texture **Sandstone**, Scaling **100%**, Relief **15**, Lighting Direction **Bottom right**

Options Stroke Length **40**, Stroke Detail **20**, Texture **Brick**, Scaling **50%**, Relief **30**, Lighting Direction **Left**

Rough Pastels Interface/Variables

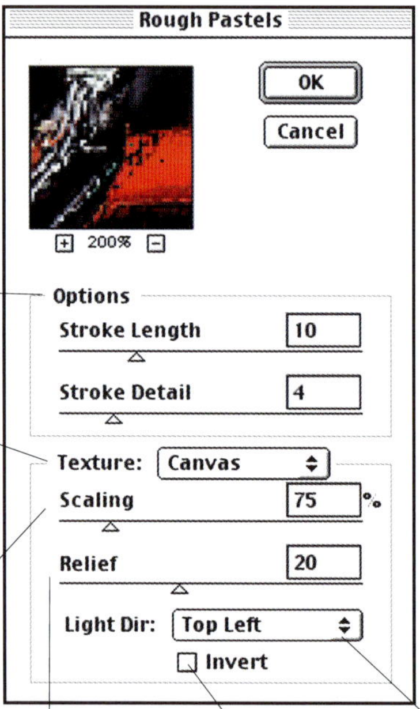

PREVIEW
The preview window is variable from 25% to 1600%. Click and hold on the preview to see the original before the filter is run

OPTIONS
Stroke Length 0–40
Stroke Detail 1–20

TEXTURE
(Four preset textures – the user can create their own)
Brick, Burlap, Canvas, Sandstone, Load Texture

SCALING
(The scale of the pattern or texture)
50%–200%

RELIEF
(Depth or height of texture)
0–50

INVERT TEXTURE
(Recesses the texture when inverted)

LIGHTING DIRECTION
(Top, Right, Bottom, Left, Top right, etc)

Options Stroke Length **6**
Stroke Detail **4**
Texture **Canvas**
Scaling **100%**
Relief **20**
Lighting Direction **Bottom**

The Paint Alchemy filter will react to the amount of information of the original image. More intricate areas of the original will result in detailed sketching, while softer, less detailed areas of the original will give loose areas in the finished filtered image.

For this pastel sketch of a Venetian gondola scene Adobe's Rough Pastel filter was run, holding image detail while applying a Sandstone texture. The filter accurately replicates pastel work and the image can then be used as the base for further work.

Options Stroke Length **25**
Stroke Detail **10**
Texture **Sandstone**
Scaling **200%**
Relief **10**
Lighting direction **Top Left**

This rough pastel sketch of a field of yellow poppies uses expressive pastel strokes to imply a sense of movement. Two plug-ins were used to create the image. Xaos Tools' Paint Alchemy was run to give a base artwork of colour and tonal areas with very little detail. The Adobe Rough Pastel filter was run over this to give a stronger paper texture.

X RES

Photoshop

Illustrator

PhotoDeluxe

Painter

Art Dabbler

Drawing Tablet

Oil pastel with a tablet

Oil pastels are dense in texture, with the oil base giving the medium viscosity and adding substance to the marks made on the paper or canvas. It is possible to blend colours with great subtlety, giving flexibility and control. However, the medium also lends itself to working quickly, sketching in areas of colour and tone, with detail being added later with fine pastels or pencil.

Stylus pressure
The pastel marks become heavier and denser by varying the pressure on the stylus. Oil pastel tends to fill-in when used heavily, with little paper grain showing through.

Smudging
Oil pastel can be blended by smudging line work with a finger or torchon. The digital artist can simulate this effect by using a wet brush to move and soften marks.

Working on textured papers
Experiment with creating paper texture using pastels, or try working with a limited palette of colours and using a tinted base paper.

Blending
Using short, controlled marks it is possible to create gradual colour changes. The colour was changed from red to yellow and blended by varying through a range of oranges.

Crosshatching
Crosshatching techniques work effectively with all pastels and are an easy and effective way of laying in large areas of tone.

Pointillist
Optical colour mixing occurs when short marks or dots are used to create a pattern and it is left to the viewer's eye to decipher the image.

Soft tones
A large, soft brush with little pressure applied to the stylus simulates the effects of using the side of a pastel stick.

Heavy pastel marks
The digital artist can simulate depth by working with vibrant or opposing colours and running a Lighting filter to define areas where colours meet.

DETAIL
Glass objects can be made to look three-dimensional by the careful placing of highlights. On rounded objects, such as this bottle, the light bouncing off the glass should follow the contours of the form and have a diffused edge.

This detailed still life study in oil pastel shows the depth of colour and tone that can be achieved when working with Painter's tools. Working from a reference photograph, oil pastel brushes were used to draw directly over the original image. Colour was selected from the photograph using the eyedropper tool.

Tips

- A trick used by real media pastel artists is to follow the shape of an object with the marks made by the pastel.
- Curved shapes are well suited to this technique, which greatly enhances the illusion of form and depth.

Creating Drama

This study of waves crashing on a beach uses traditional oil pastel techniques to great effect. Loose, short pastel marks add to the image's feeling of movement and drama, and give the impression of colours and tones being mixed on the paper. This optical mixing technique was used most famously by the pointillist artist Georges Seurat in the 19th century.

This moody monochrome study is of the same beach scene. The image was coloured blue using Photoshop's Hue and Saturation controls. Once blue, the colour balance was altered to add reds to the shadows and yellows to the highlights. An overall tan paper was added and then the piece taken into MetaCreations Painter, where pastel and pencil marks were drawn in. Finally, the Unsharp Mask was run to retrieve detail.

Oil pastel plug-ins

Oil pastel techniques vary greatly from artist to artist but the properties of the medium remain the same – an oily texture that lends itself to effective colour mixing. The texture of the pastels tends to build up and fill-in on the paper where rough pastels would show more grain.

The advantage the digital oil pastel has over real pastel is the infinite range of colours available. Subtle variations in shading can be achieved, not only with pressure sensitive tools, but also by sampling a range of colours from an existing image.

Options Stroke Length **10**
Highlight Area **15**
Intensity **5**

Options Stroke Length **5**
Highlight Area **15**
Intensity **0**

Smudge Stick Interface/ Variables

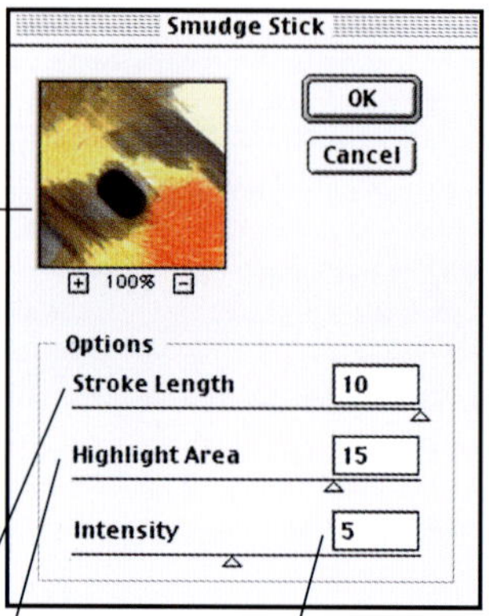

PREVIEW
The preview window is variable from 25% to 1600%. Click and hold on the preview to see the original before the filter is run

Options

STROKE LENGTH
(The length image pixels will be smudged)
0–10

HIGHLIGHT AREA
(Overall brightness of the image is affected, with low numbers giving a darker result)
0–20

INTENSITY
(How strong the filter is. High numbers can be overpowering, although the Fade filter command can be used to tone down the results)
0–10

Options Stroke Length **10**
Highlight Area **5**
Intensity **5**

Options Stroke Length **3**
Highlight Area **20**
Intensity **0**

SMOOTH LINES
To achieve realistic oil pastel work vary the sizes of the brushes used. This mimics soft oil pastel, losing any sharp edges.

INTENSE COLOUR
Increasing the saturation of the original image will give the filter more to work with and will result in more depth of colour on the finished image.

The Adobe Smudge Stick filter gives the closest results to oil pastel work. It helps to first slightly soften and brighten the image before running the filter. To regain detail after the filter has been run use Photoshop's Fade filter command – with the preview checked you can see the results as you move the slider.

Tips

A soft paper grain was added to the finished images of the cockatoo.

- Adobe's Grain filter (Filter, Texture, Grain) was run and set to soft. This adds texture and helps to blend colours and tones together more realistically.
- The Grain filter gives several options for textures that can be generated and added to artwork after completion. These include Soft, Crumpled, Contrasty and Stippled.
- The other variables are the filters Intensity and Contrast.

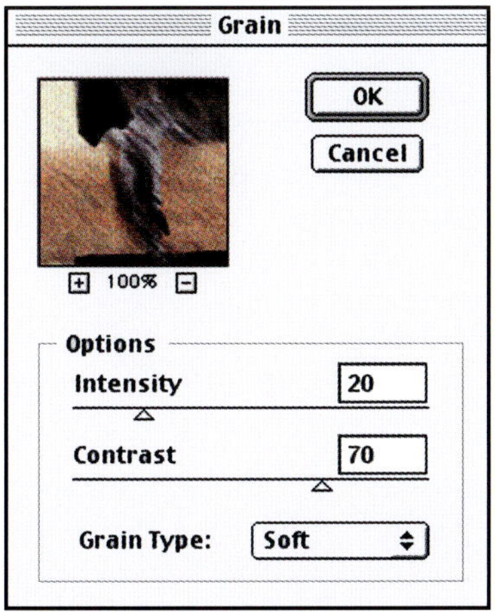

Grain filter
The Grain filter is most useful for adding texture to flat images. Run at low settings to add grain and slight colour variations to the artwork.

Paint Alchemy

Xaos Tools' Paint Alchemy filter was run on this image of a cockatoo using the standard settings that came with the plug-in. The pastel strokes are non-directional and blend together softly. There are many variables for the filter, which include Pastel Size, Colour and Tone and Stroke Direction. These can be varied by the image's brightness/darkness, colour, or can be set to give random results. Experimenting with the variables can give very realistic oil pastel work.

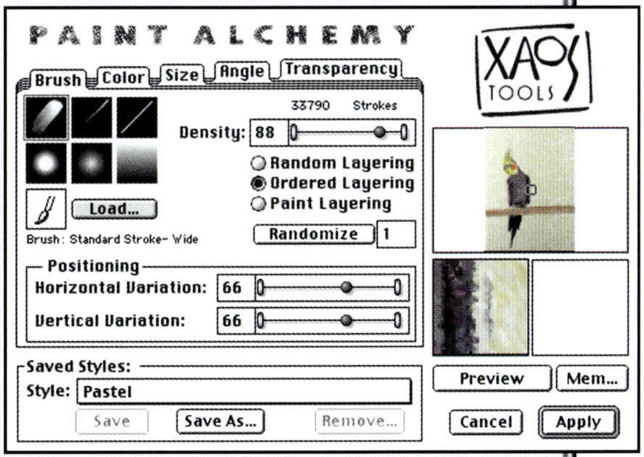

X RES
Photoshop
Illustrator
PhotoDeluxe
Painter
Art Dabbler
ColorIt
CorelDRAW
CorelPAINT
LivePIX
FreeHand

Airbrush techniques

The airbrush gained great popularity in the 1960s and '70s when its main purpose was in photo retouching, making it, in some ways, the precursor to the computer, and software such as Photoshop. The computer artist's airbrush is far more sophisticated than the real thing. The digital airbrush doesn't spit or splatter, even pressure is very simple, and laying areas of flat colour simply requires the press of a button.

THE TECHNIQUES

The key to successful airbrush illustration lies in making masks, which are used to restrict colour to certain areas of the image. Digital masking techniques are very sophisticated, allowing the artist to use transparency in the mask.

Varying ink flow through pressure
The density of paint is increased by applying pressure to the stylus, giving more saturated tones. Pressure variables include ink flow, size of brush, and differing colour.

Fading
The airbrush can be set to fade to transparent after a set distance. Higher settings give longer strokes with a soft fade out. The same variable can be set to change the paint colour from two-selected colour.

Spheres
Using a mask to stop paint bleeding beyond the circle, and a soft brush with a low opacity, this sphere was slowly built up using darker tones of the same colour.

Gradations
Perfect gradations between two colours are very difficult to achieve by conventional methods. This grade was created with Photoshop's linear gradient tool.

This airbrush image of a car was an exercise in producing accurate masks. Once each area had been masked the airbrush work was very quick, often involving filters rather than using the airbrush tool. The Blur filters, in particular, create very realistic soft airbrushing.

Faux lighting effects
A spotlit background was created over a red panel using Photoshop's Lighting Effects filter.

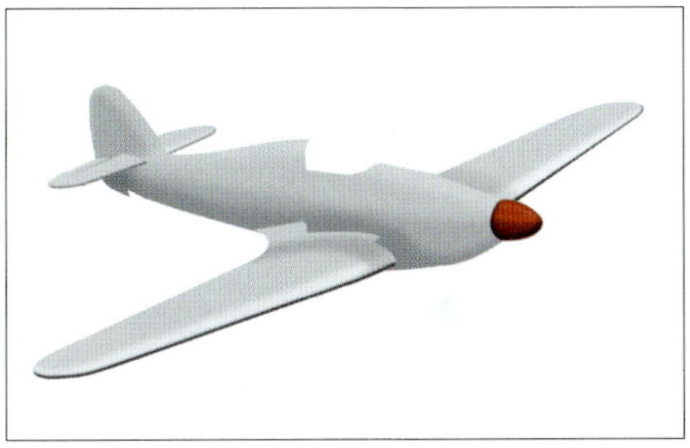

1 This image of a World War II Hurricane fighter plane was created using the airbrush techniques described opposite.

The basic shapes of the plane were masked out. Tone and form were airbrushed in using a neutral grey, as colour would be airbrushed over the top.

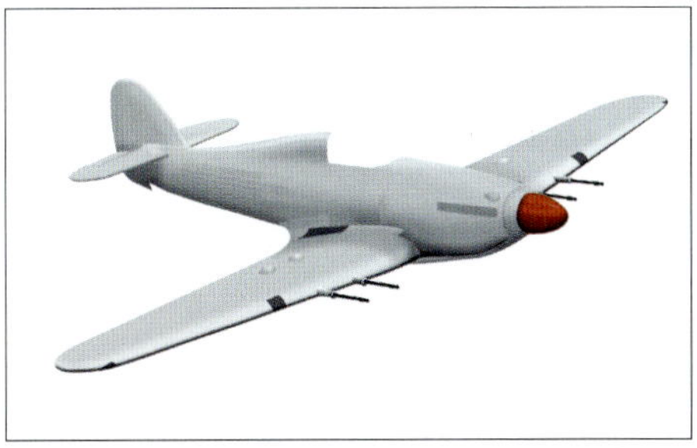

2 More detailed monochrome work was added to the basic body shape.

Aircraft are popular with airbrush artists as the medium works well with subjects that lend themselves to smooth transitions of tone.

3 The airbrush mode was changed from normal to colour; this does not affect the tone but will replace the colour of the underlying image. The paint and the markings were added.

4 The sky was brushed in with a soft airbrush, which was further softened using Blur filters. The machine gun highlights were airbrushed using the technique of painting along paths. The brushes were decreased in size and the paint colour changed from red, through yellow, to white.

Custom brushes

A greyscale image of a sphere was loaded as a custom brush. Clicking on the image creates instant bubbles.

Glowing objects

Photoshop's airbrush can be made to precisely follow a path that can be drawn with the pen tool. This glowing circle began as a path drawn in Photoshop. A large, soft brush was used, with the airbrush set to a low opacity in Multiply mode. The path is airbrushed around, reducing the size of the brush, and lightening the paint before again airbrushing around the path. This method is repeated until the desired effect is achieved.

X RES
Photoshop
Illustrator
PhotoDeluxe
Painter
Art Dabbler
Drawing Tablet

Watercolour with a tablet

To achieve a realistic watercolour painting the digital artist needs to understand the qualities of this most popular of mediums. Watercolour is applied in washes of colour, usually on white paper, with dark areas being built up with layers of successive washes. Successful watercolours should be spontaneous and delicate, although the artwork should also have depth.

Watercolour's fluidity and transparency sets it apart from other painting mediums, and the great watercolour artists throughout history have used these qualities for maximum effect. The digital painter can layer colour with electronic tools and composing methods to copy the traditional artist with great results.

THE TABLET

The stylus gives the artist great control over watercolour work. Pressure variables include paint transparency, colour, bleed and tone. The size of the brush can also be varied by the application of pressure on the stylus. The digital artist also has the power to take any watercolour paper and apply its surface to the finished artwork.

TECHNIQUES

These watercolour techniques were created in MetaCreations Painter, which has powerful and realistic tools for this medium. Wet-in-wet techniques are easy to achieve with a Water Diffuse brush.

Flat wash colour
A large flat brush was used to paint an even tone, which should vary slightly and build up towards the edge of the brush. The paper's key reacts to the paint being applied.

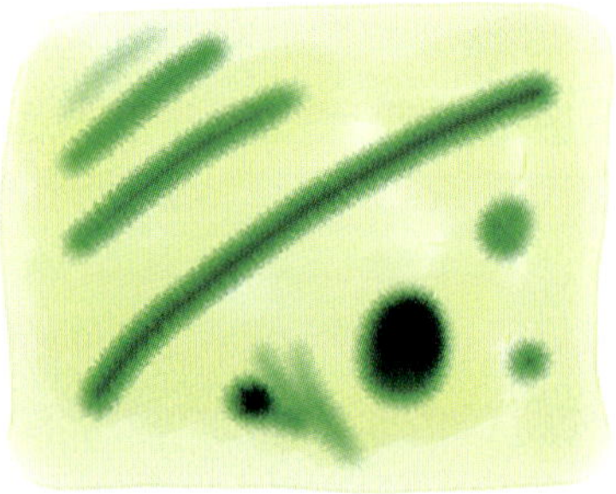

Wet-in-wet
This technique replicates painting a colour over a wet wash. The green paint bleeds dramatically into the yellow background.

Gradated tone
To achieve a gradated background apply a slightly darker tone to a dry wash. A strong watercolour paper texture was applied to the final gradation.

Lifting colour
While the background is still wet it is possible to remove some of the colour from the blue wash using a water only brush.

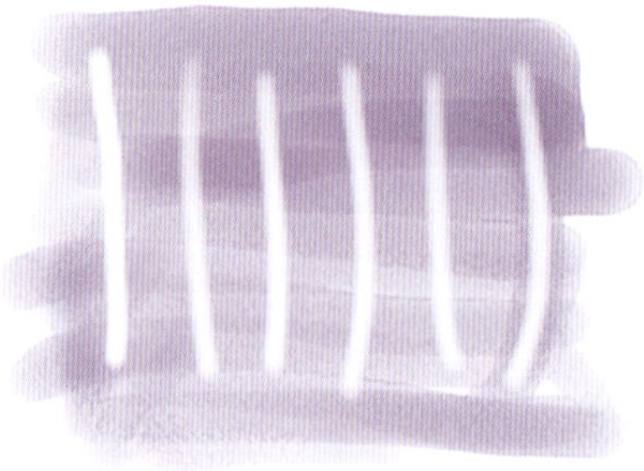

Wet eraser
An eraser was used on this wet purple wash. Highlights can be picked out of flat tone by using the stylus lightly.

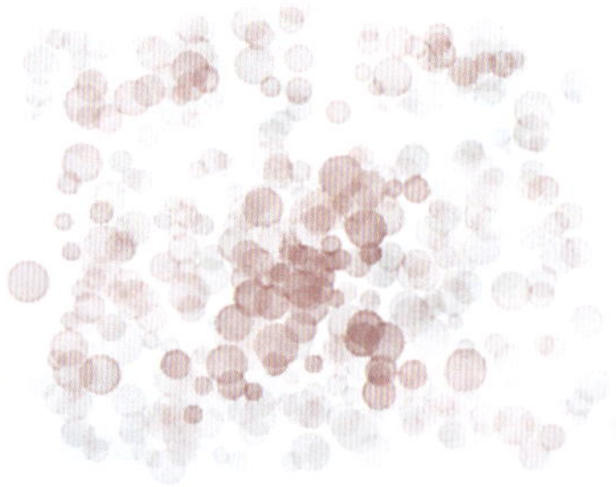

Spatter paint
Painter has a watercolour brush that mimics flicking a normal paintbrush. The amount of spatter can be controlled by the speed of the stylus.

Crosshatching

Crosshatching, and other pattern-making techniques, work particularly well in watercolour. The transparent nature of the medium lends itself to building up detailed areas from delicate crosshatching.

Drying and colour washing

An area of flat yellow was painted onto a heavily textured watercolour paper. The artwork was dried, and then painted with a dark orange, varying the pressure to allow more or less yellow to show through.

This detailed study of a stargazer lily was painted using a small brush, carefully building up colour and tone using crosshatching techniques. A muted colour palette and delicate, precise brushwork produced a very realistic painting.

Watercolour Plug-Ins

The two images above are examples of the Adobe watercolour filter set to show the differing effects achievable. Although the filter does produce usable and interesting effects it is very difficult to capture the subtleties of translucency and lightness that real watercolour work yields. The filter tends to darken the image overall and lays the washes in an awkward and clumsy way.

Tips

- Start your drawing by running a pencil filter and add watercolour work on top.
- Build up colour by overlaying washes from light to dark.
- Experiment with different paper textures: slight changes to the paper surface can make a dramatic difference to the final work.
- Highlights can be added using a lighter colour than the base, a technique that is almost impossible with real watercolours.
- Drama can be expressed with free brushwork. Experiment with your stylus brush tracking controls.

Step-by-step watercolour technique

The following steps show a typical way of working using Painter to create a watercolour landscape. This is a guide to only one method – the techniques should be as individual as the artist making the painting. The reference photograph was used as a starting point, but a spontaneous, painterly effect was the aim, as opposed to a detailed study.

Consider the way a conventional watercolour painter would build up tone using subtle colour washes. Aim to achieve layers of transparency similar to the properties of great watercolour paintings.

1 A rough pencil drawing of outlines and shapes was made using a soft 2B pencil. The sketch was very quick and would be used as reference when laying colour washes.

A landscape photograph was scanned as reference for this study, correcting the image for colour and brightness using the Intellihance filter. Once happy with the colour, the image was resized to the final size of the painting and saved as a TIFF file.

Tips

One way of ensuring accuracy is to create the master sketch using a copy of the scanned image and running a sketch filter. Once the desired drawing is achieved it can be overlaid on the tonal watercolour study.

- Set the Layers Blending mode to overlay and the sketch will lighten and darken the paint, adding detail without overpowering the delicate colour work.
- This technique works equally well with other painting and drawing methods. Some interesting brushwork can be achieved by combining different drawing methods with various paint techniques.

4 Texture was added into the foreground using a very fine watercolour brush and a burnt umber colour. A sense of movement in the wheat was achieved by very subtle brushwork that was frequently overpainted to lose some of the detail painted in earlier. Detail was added into the trees with a wet brush.

2 Soft colour washes were laid, sampling colours from the original image and using a large watercolour brush that reacted with the paper's key. Areas of tone and colour were washed in to give a very basic colour sketch. As watercolour relies on building up tone from light to dark, the colours were kept pale and soft. Finally, this paint layer was dried; washes overlaid would then not affect the dried paint but would overlay and darken.

3 Shape and form were gradually built up through soft colour washes. Finer brushes were used for more detail around the building and trees. To create detail in the foreground a water only brush was used to lift out some of the colour, adding detail in the grass areas. Darker tones of grey were used to add depth below the trees.

5 Detail was painted onto the building's doors and windows and texture was added to the treetops, using dark greens and umbers. Using Painter's Dodge and Burn tools, areas were painted to give a sense of drama to the lighting. The final step was to rerun the paper texture surface control to retrieve the watercolour paper texture. One of the most important skills when using watercolour is knowing when to stop – overworking an image can easily spoil a painting, with colours becoming muddy and lifeless. This study was deliberately kept loose, capturing the feel of the setting rather than concentrating on detail.

Oil with a tablet

The range of oil techniques is as immense as the number of artists who have used this ancient medium. Oils can be used straight from the tube to give solid or heavily textured impasto paint, or can be diluted to give a fluid smoothness to the paint surface.

TECHNIQUES

Experimentation is the key to finding techniques that are pleasing to you and the viewer; look for inspiration from other painting styles – pen and ink drawing techniques using oil paint can be beautiful.

Try to build your repertoire of paint techniques based around the qualities of the medium, its viscosity and fluidity when blended, or for more drama, use thick paint in bold slabs where the viewer will optically mix the paint. The swatches show just some of the techniques possible with MetaCreations Painter.

Alla prima
Short strokes of colour are blended together to give a 'first attempt' at a drawing. Use blocks of colour to rough in areas of colour and tone.

Blending
Blend one colour into another using a soft brush. The colours will mix to give intermediary tones. Vary the direction and weight of the brushwork.

Broken colour
Using short but fluid brushstrokes, optically blend two colours by pattern making. Interesting tonal effects can be accomplished with this technique.

Stippling
This is another form of broken colour, and involves applying the paint using the end of the brush to make spots on the canvas. Tap randomly with the stylus, trying not to draw strokes, to make different weights of spot.

Dry brush
This shows the effect of using a brush that has very little paint loaded onto it. The paper or canvas texture shows through the paint, while lightening the stylus pressure breaks up the strokes even more.

Glazing
The effect of glazing in oil paint can easily be copied using a transparent brush. The yellow colour is overpainted with a blue glaze; the yellow should show through and mix with the blue to give differing tones.

Gradations
Soft non-directional brushwork is used to build up a gradation from light to dark green. Continue overpainting until the desired smoothness is achieved.

Wet-in-wet
Mixing two oils with Painter's Distorto brush gives the feel of mixing two wet oil colours together. The paint should not mix properly and the colours should move together, giving the look of oils repelling each other.

Textures
Using different brushes, or applying scanned textures, can add interest to a painting. Here the Scratchboard tool was used to create an interesting brush effect.

Scratching out
To copy the painter's technique of scratching paint off the surface of the canvas the Scratchboard pen tool was used, with white paint selected then scratched with directional rapid pen strokes.

EYEBROWS
Detail was painted in using very small brushes and was built up hair by hair.

EYES
Brushwork was kept subtle and simple. With direct eye contact it is important to capture a liveliness in the eyes.

SKIN TONES
The skin tones were painted with loose brushwork to give the portrait a relaxed feel. The skin colours were sampled from the original using the eyedropper tool.

SHADOW AREAS
Shadows were built up using overlays of slightly transparent colour.

HIGHLIGHTS
Highlight areas were painted in towards completion of the painting. Photoshop's Dodge tool was used to very subtly lighten the highlight areas.

This portrait study in oils began as an image on a Photo CD. The background was painted out to eliminate distracting detail and the jumper's colour was changed to black. Various oil brushes and painterly techniques were used to achieve an alla prima painting.

The image of an apple was scanned and cleaned up. Various oil brushes were used directly over the top of the scan, colours being picked using the eyedropper tool. Once the shape, colour and tone were roughed in more detail was added by using short, broken colour brushwork.

Photoshop

Step-by-step oil technique

This motorbike was painted by building up shape, tone and colour until the image was roughed in. Working over this skeleton, light and shadow areas were defined, giving the bike form. Finally, detail was added using small brushes and the Smudge tool. The image was then composed with a sky that had been painted for another project.

PHOTOSHOP'S SMUDGE TOOL

A powerful tool when any painterly style is required, the Smudge tool in Photoshop can be used when blending colours. Set the smudge preferences to a low percentage and the tool will mix colours, giving the appearance of thick paint with a low viscosity. Colour can be pulled or pushed into areas, creating a realistic painterly feel.

1 A mask was created for the body panel of the bike to stop paint from spilling over to other parts of the painting. Tone and colour were roughed in with a broad, flat brush. This should be done very quickly, simply indicating light, shade and shape.

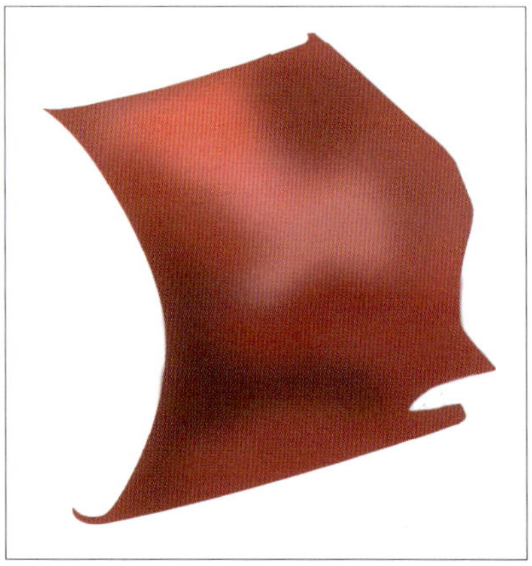

2 Once the panel has been roughed in the gradations of tone can be smoothed using Photoshop's blur filters. A Motion Blur was used, with an angle of 45° and 30 pixels. The filter was run again with the angle changed from 45° to 0°. This softened blending between light and dark areas.

3 More detail was added in shadow areas using Photoshop's Dodge and Burn tools. These tools darken or lighten areas, while retaining the colour of the underlying image. Careful work with small but soft brushes built up the shape, form and tone of the body panel.

4 Final detail was worked over the panel by applying colour with a small brush. Colour was pushed around the image to give highlights and shadow using the Smudge tool with a very small, soft brush and settings of 100%.

The sky was painted using soft brushes, blending colour and tone with the Smudge tool. The Adobe Distort Shear filter was used to bend the sky in the middle of the horizon.

Glass in the headlights was painted with a small brush, using a broken colour technique to add texture and form.

Final detail was added with fine pencil, brush and airbrushes, using careful masking techniques to hold sharp edges around the metalwork.

Larger tonal areas were loosely brushed in with a paintbrush, which was then filtered with the Adobe Paint Daubs filter run at a low setting.

5 The whole image of the bike was painted using this technique, with each section carefully masked out and then painted in. Care was taken to ensure that detail was retained while the feel of the paint was loose and free.

Tips

Photoshop's Smudge tool is invaluable when copying oil painting techniques.

- Set at 100% and, using a small soft brush, smudge colour around to create detail.
- Set at 50%, with a large soft brush, and blend tonal work to give soft gradations.
- Copy from other layers in a multilayered document and smudge. Parts of the image below are copied onto the working image.

Oil plug-ins

There are a number of plug-ins bundled with Photoshop that emulate real media painting, and oil painting in particular. Experiment with all the paint plug-ins, as they can be invaluable for providing a base or underpainting to be worked over. Scans, for example, can be instantly changed into a colour sketch that can be used as the basis of a painting.

Plug-in Adobe Paint Daubs
The Paint Daubs filter gives a realistic painterly brush feel. Use it directly on an unmodified image to hold image detail while implying brushwork, or try modifying the image first by blurring or painting out some of the detail to give the final work a loose and free style.

Paint Daubs Interface/ Variables

Options
BRUSH SIZE
Variable 1–50

SHARPNESS
Variable 0–40

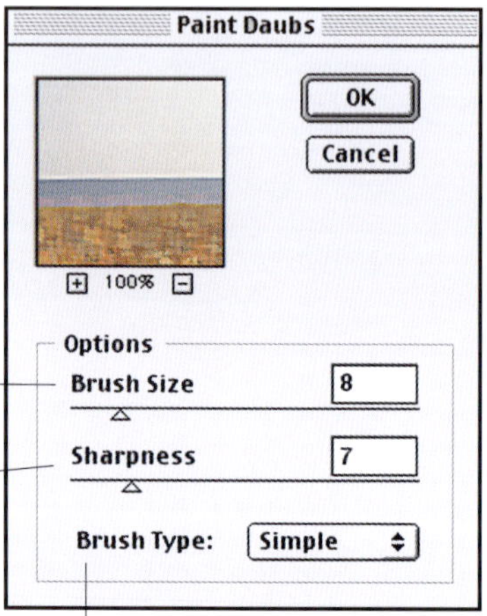

BRUSH TYPE
Simple, Light Rough, Dark Rough, Wide Sharp, Wide blurry, Sparkle.
Selecting a different type of brush greatly changes the appearance of the final artwork. The rough brushes change the overall tone, while the wide brushes give loose results.

Options
Brush Size **10**
Sharpness **10**
Type **Simple**

Options
Brush Size **20**
Sharpness **10**
Type **Dark Rough**

Options
Brush Size **20**
Sharpness **25**
Type **Wide Blurry**

Options
Brush Size **27**
Sharpness **7**
Type **Sparkle**

Plug-in Adobe Palette Knife
The Palette Knife filter replicates painting with oils using a palette knife. Image detail is greatly reduced and the results are loose, with broad painterly strokes. This filter is effective when creating a base artwork that can be painted over to re-establish detail.

Options Stroke Size **10**
Stroke Detail **3**
Softness **5**

Options Stroke Size **20**
Stroke Detail **1**
Softness **10**

Palette Knife Interface/ Variables

Options

STROKE SIZE
Variable 1–50

STROKE DETAIL
Variable 1–3

SOFTNESS
0–10

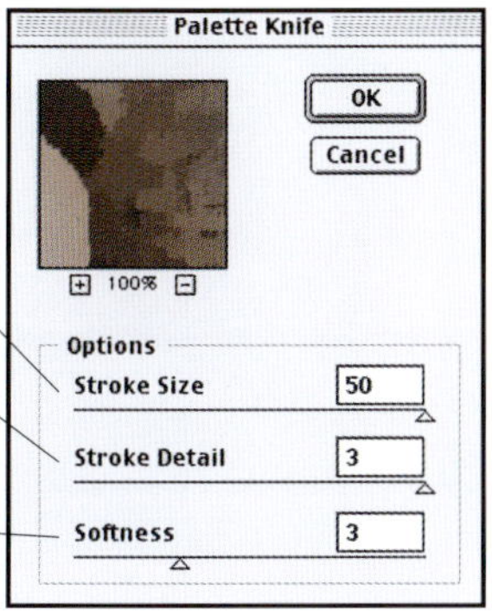

Options Stroke Size **20**
Stroke Detail **3**
Softness **0**

The extreme settings on this filter have produced an abstract form based on the original image of shells, spreading and simplifying the colour and tone of the original. A thick impasto feel can be achieved by playing with the tools.

Options Stroke Size **50**
Stroke Detail **3**
Softness **3**

TIPS

To give the paint filters more interest where there are areas of flat tone run the Add Noise filter.

- Set at a medium number and, with the Monochrome option selected, a pattern or fine grain is added to the image.
- Run the Motion Blur filter to give the grain a brushed-in look.
- Run the Paint Daubs filter to create areas of transparent colour where there was flat tone.

X RES
Photoshop
Illustrator
PhotoDeluxe
Painter
Art Dabbler
ColorIt
CorelDRAW
CorelPAINT
LivePIX

More oil plug-ins

Two further paint filters from Adobe are Dry Brush and Underpainting. Again, these are both useful for laying in the base artwork for a painting or drawing but they have the advantage of rendering a textured surface onto the artwork. The underpainting gives a roughed out painting on variable surfaces, including canvas and burlap (hessian).

Plug-in Adobe Underpainting
The Underpainting filter is a very powerful tool for creating painted artwork. Variables range from brush size to canvas texture, scale and relief. This filter is useful for creating a base artwork, as image detail tends to be lost after filtering.

Underpainting Interface/ Variables

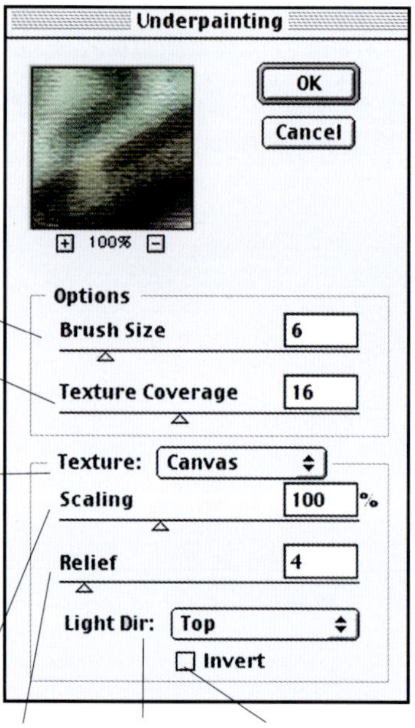

Options

BRUSH SIZE
0–40

TEXTURE COVERAGE
0–40

TEXTURE
Brick, Burlap, Canvas, Sandstone, Load texture (textures can be created as greyscale files and loaded into the filter)

SCALING
50%–200%

RELIEF
0–50

LIGHTING DIRECTION
Top
Right
Left
Bottom
Top Left
Top Right
Bottom Left
Bottom Right

INVERT
(The texture can be inverted to change it from a relief texture to a depressed texture)

Options Brush Size **6**
Texture Coverage **16**
Texture **Canvas**
Scaling **100%**
Relief **4**
Lighting Direction **Top**

Options Brush Size **10**
Texture Coverage **10**
Texture **Burlap**
Scaling **50%**
Relief **8**
Lighting Direction **Top right**

Options Brush Size **20**
Texture Coverage **10**
Texture **Sandstone**
Scaling **50%**
Relief **8**
Lighting Direction **Bottom right**
Invert

Options Brush Size **40**
Texture Coverage **20**
Texture **Burlap**
Scaling **100%**
Relief **8**
Lighting Direction **Top left**

Plug-in Adobe Dry Brush
The Dry Brush filter gives the image the appearance of being painted with a brush that has very little paint loaded up. The texture of the surface reacts with the paint leaving realistic dry brushed artwork.

Options
Brush Size **10**
Brush Detail **10**
Texture **3**

Dry Brush Interface/ Variables

Options

BRUSH SIZE
Variable 0–10

BRUSH DETAIL
0–10

TEXTURE
1–3
It is not possible to vary the texture patterns used by this filter

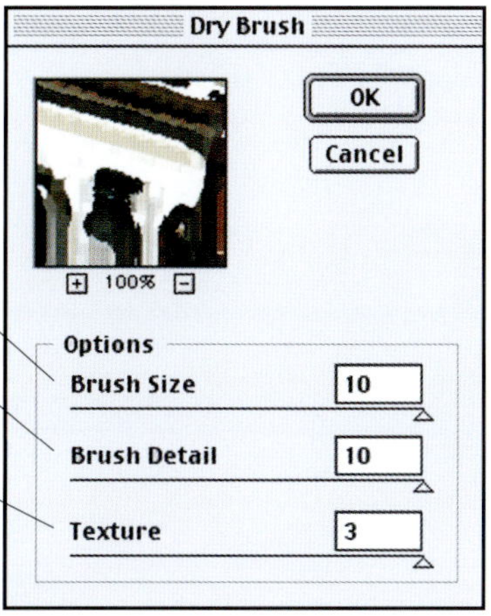

Options
Brush Size **5**
Brush Detail **5**
Texture **2**

Options
Brush Size **2**
Brush Detail **3**
Texture **1**

TIPS

When using a painterly plug-in it can become very obvious to the viewer that all brushstrokes are going in the same direction. This can look unrealistic, as real painters tend to vary brush direction and weight.

- To avoid this problem, flip the image and run the filter, then flip the filtered artwork back. The brushwork will be going in the opposite direction.
- This can be done on the component parts of the image as well. Run the filter on each individual channel of an RGB image, first on the Red channel, then vary the filter's setting slightly and run on the Green channel. Finally, flip the Blue channel, run the filter and flip it back again.

Options Brush Size **1**
Brush Detail **1**
Texture **1**

More digital tools

These pages show some examples of the vast range of filters available to the digital artist. Some may appear to be too quirky to be of any use, but remember that filters can be run on small selections within artwork.

This is an effective way of utilizing the more extreme filters while keeping their effects subtle and usable. It is also possible to run the filters on selection masks and then apply them to the image, giving a subtle effect.

Adobe Poster Edges

Adobe Crosshatch

Adobe Cut Out

Adobe Spatter

Adobe Ink Outlines

Adobe Crystallize

Adobe Colour Halftone

Tips

- Many filters can be used to create a size or paper texture that can then be applied to a finished artwork. The Crumple, Noise and Blur filters produce interesting textures.
- Treating a series of images that need to print together with similar filters unifies the images into a set. Try running Lighting Effects filters with soft directional light to give several images the same feel.
- Hard-edged masks can look severe when painting subjects that have soft transitions in colour and tone. After drawing a mask run a filter to alter or soften the mask. More natural artwork results are achieved using this technique.
- By running different filters on sections of a painting a collage effect can be created. Layering differently filtered images over one another produces interesting results.
- Images can be created by applying different textures to selected areas of the artwork. Subtle and delicate drawing can be achieved.
- Upon completion of any digital artwork it is good practice to run the Unsharp Mask filter. This sharpens any detail lost while painting or filtering. The resulting image will have more clarity and depth, and printing results will be greatly improved.

Adobe Pointillize

Adobe Mezzotint

Adobe Stamp

Adobe Photocopy

Adobe Find Edges

Adobe Solarize

Adobe Texturizer

Adobe Tiles

Xenofex Crumple

Adobe Patchwork

Eye Candy Antimatter

Adobe Trace Contour

Eye Candy Jiggle

Eye Candy Fur

Kai Power Tools 3 Smudge

Eye Candy Swirl

Kai Power Tools 3 Glass Lens

Eye Candy Squint

Kai Power Tools 5 Frax Flame

Eye Candy Water Drops

Inklination Pen and Ink Crosshatching

X RES

Photoshop

Illustrator

PhotoDeluxe

Painter

Art Dabbler

ColorIt

CorelDRAW

CorelPAINT

LivePIX

Kai Power Tools 5 Radwarp

Adobe Reticulation

Kai Power Tools 5 Blurrr

Adobe Plaster

Kai Power Tools 3 Twirl

Adobe Note Paper

Adobe Conté Crayon

Adobe Emboss

Treatments for finished artwork

The digital artist can replicate effects and treatments that exist in the real world after the artwork has been completed. Effects can range from ageing and staining artwork, spot lighting images and scratching the surface. To age the overall colour and tone within the image, slightly desaturate using Photoshop's Hue and Saturation controls. Ageing the surface of an oil painting by cracking the varnish, and softening the square edges of digital artwork are demonstrated here.

Soft frames

All digital paint and image software utilizes a rectangular painting area. Watercolour artists will often choose not to fill all the paper, giving a softer brushed edge to their work. There are filters that can create soft painterly or graphic edges in your artwork. Alternatively, you can paint out the unwanted areas with white paint and a soft watercolour brush. Here, the Extensis Photoframe was used to add a soft watercolour border to the image of flowers in a field.

EXTENSIS PHOTOFRAME

The PhotoFrame interface allows the user to vary the effects of the border's angle, size, blur, and opacity. Three separate borders can be combined with all of Photoshop's blending modes. The borders are greyscale files that are supplied with the software, or can be created by the artist.

The Photoframe filter was run with a watercolour border and a canvas border, both supplied with Photoframe. The opacity was kept at 100% but the watercolour border was blurred to soften the edges even more.

CRAQUELURE

Craquelure is the name given to the fine cracks that appear on the surface of an oil painting. With oil paints the surface can suffer, over many years, from the adverse effects of humidity, heat and shrinkage, leaving an overall pattern of tiny cracks. With image manipulation software this effect can be copied for instant ageing.

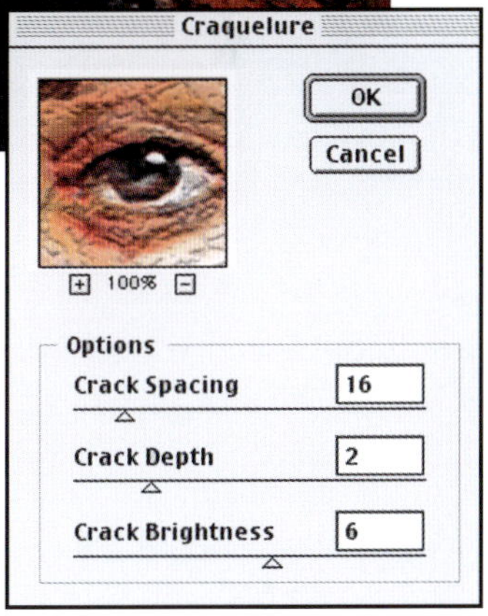

Craquelure Interface/Variables
The Craquelure filter from Adobe replicates the cracked surface of an old painting. Variables include the space and depth of the cracks, as well as their brightness.

Mixed media work with plug-ins

An advantage the digital painter has over his real media contemporary is the ability to work with a variety of paint and drawing mediums within the same composition. Mixing oil and watercolour would be very difficult, if not impossible, with real techniques but is simple when using electronic paints and pencils. Work can be overlaid and given transparency at the same time – thick, impasto paint could be made transparent, for example, allowing a delicate pencil drawing to show through.

The possibilities are endless and experimentation is the key when mixing media; happy accidents can often lead to stunning results.

THE TECHNIQUES

These examples show some of the possibilities when mixing styles and techniques – all the work was completed using filters. The final images were composed using different blending methods, or by selectively allowing certain areas of one image to blend into others.

1 This image of a building was chosen for a graphic treatment, because the building's form and tones were very simple, with strong defining lines and shapes.

2 The Adobe Cut Out filter was run to simplify the image to flat areas of colour. This filter produces effects similar to Matisse's later cut paper work.

3 The Inklination crosshatching pen and ink filter was run on another copy of the image. A graphic black and white pen image resulted.

4 The two were composited using Photoshop's Multiply Blending mode, adding the line work to the flat areas of colour. By lowering the layer's opacity the pen marks took on colour. The final image is an interesting mix of coloured pen work and flat gouache-like areas of colour.

TIPS

- Interesting results can often be achieved when mixing an artistic filtered image with one that has been treated in a graphic way. The graphic can work as the basic drawing or sketch, with the paint adding emotional impact or accentuating areas of the final image.

1 This image of a cat demonstrates how to focus the viewer's attention on one area of the image.

2 The image was sketched as loose coloured pencil work using Xaos Tools' Paint Alchemy filter and with the soft coloured pencil preset.

3 The Adobe Paint Daubs filter was then run with a large brush setting. This gave the image a painterly effect, while adding detail.

4 The final image uses Photoshop's Layer masks to paint the cat into the pencil image. The final step was to bring in the original photo and, again using Layer masks, brush in the cat's face, the focal point of the study.

Combining Two Painting Styles

This image began with two copies of the lamp, running a different drawing and painting filter on each. The two were combined by dragging one onto the other in Photoshop to create a two-layer document. The upper layer was selected and the Blending mode changed to Multiply, which adds the upper layer's tonal values to the lower image. This darkened the image, so the top layer's opacity was reduced to brighten the image and allow more of the underlying layer to appear.

We treated three copies of this still life image in very different styles. The Adobe Halftone filter was applied to the image, right, creating a graphic black and white scene. In Photoshop, the image is layered with pointillist and oil paint layers to create the painting below.

The layered images were mixed together using Photoshop's Layer masks, with the halftone serving as a stark backdrop for the painterly images. The pointillist image was painted in around the table and fruit, before painting the thick oil paint image onto the fruit bowls.

Photoshop

Plug-ins

Creating a digital woodcut

Woodcut and other relief printing techniques have been in use since printing began. The digital artist has the power to re-create these time consuming processes with the press of a few buttons. Dramatic results can be achieved in a very short space of time and this gives the artist great opportunities to experiment. Other print techniques, such as intaglio, linocut and scratchboard can be re-created by varying the settings used here.

This digital woodcut was created in Photoshop, but the technique can easily be used by other imaging programs that run Photoshop-compatible plug-ins. The High Pass filter is designed to remove shading in an image and accentuate areas where a sharp colour transition occurs, emphasizing bright areas, particularly highlights.

1 To begin, the image was cropped and colour corrected (see page 29 Preparing Scanned Images). A duplicate of the image was floated above the original. The layer was copied by dragging it onto the New Layer icon at the bottom of the Layers palette.

2 The High Pass filter (Filter, Other, High Pass) was run with a setting of 10. This created a relief of the original image, which still contained tone and some colour.

Tips

- Play around with the blending modes in the Layers palette. Whole new images and effects appear by just changing the mode and the Layer's opacity. Adjusting the sliders in the Layers palette submenu will allow different areas of the colour image to show through. Again, experiment until you find the result you want.

3 The contrast was increased, bringing out detail in the leaves and background, and the image desaturated to remove all colour. The relief image was then posterized (Image, Adjust, Posterize) and the levels set at 2. This gave a black and white 'woodcut' of the original image.

4 The black and white image was then layered over the original colour version. The Blending mode was changed to Multiply in the Layers palette to add the blacks of the upper image to the colour and tone of the base image.

5 The final step was to slightly desaturate the colour using Photoshop's Hue and Saturation controls. To finish, the image was flattened and saved as a TIFF file.

RAPID RESULTS
The final image was created in a very short space of time. The real media equivalent would take far longer and the artist would have to be happy with the composition from the start.

Taking it Further

Photoshop

Xaos

Using masks for dramatic effect

This image started life as a transparency of a church on a sunny summer's day. The mood was changed dramatically by replacing the blue sky with a stormy night scene, while the churchyard is bathed in bright daylight. The work of surrealist painter René Magritte provided the inspiration for this artwork.

Objective To create drama by replacing the sky in an image

Teaching Points

1 Adding canvas areas to image

2 Selecting the sky

3 Replacement and special effects

2 The sky was selected by painting a mask with Photoshop's Quick Mask mode. This selection mask is simply black and white. White areas represent holes in the mask that can be edited, while black areas are completely masked out and cannot be worked on.

1 The shape of the image was changed by adding canvas at the top. In Photoshop, Menu→Image→Canvas Size was selected, where options are given in a dialogue box. The size was increased by 150% and extra canvas added by selecting the appropriate Anchor square.

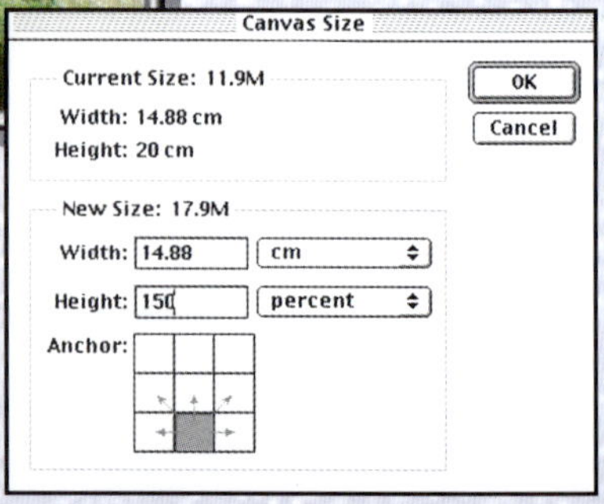

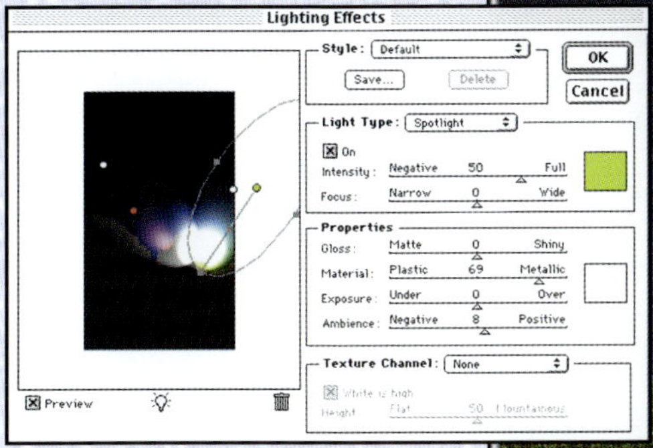

3 To create a dark, stormy sky the Quick Mask was loaded as a selection and the area was filled with a deep blue colour. The spotlighted areas around the church were added with the Photoshop Lighting Effects filter.

The Add Noise filter was run to give the sky texture

Three spotlights, aimed from different directions, and with varying colours, were used to create highlights

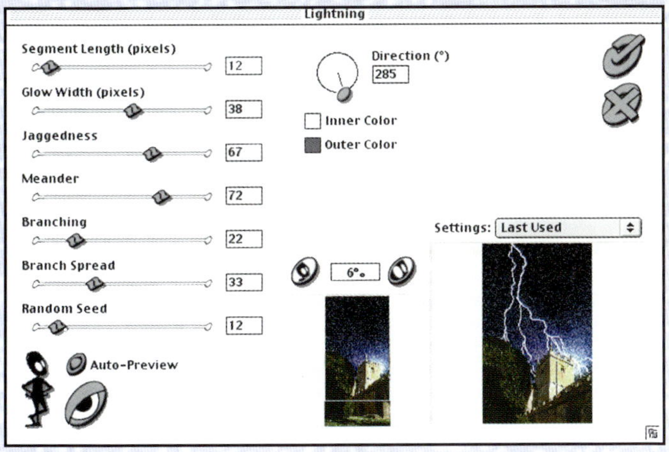

4 The bolt of lightning was added to the sky using Xenofex Lightning filter. The many variables were explored until the desired lightning bolt effect was achieved.

5 A copy was made of the image and the Adobe Underpainting filter was run. This adds canvas texture and begins to give the image a painterly quality. On another copy of the image the Xaos Tools' Paint Alchemy filter was run, with the Oil Canvas Detail preset. This produced a more natural paint quality, with variable brushstrokes. The two painterly images were copied back onto the original by dragging one image to another with the moving tool. The layered document now contained the master image, the underpainting and the oil painting.

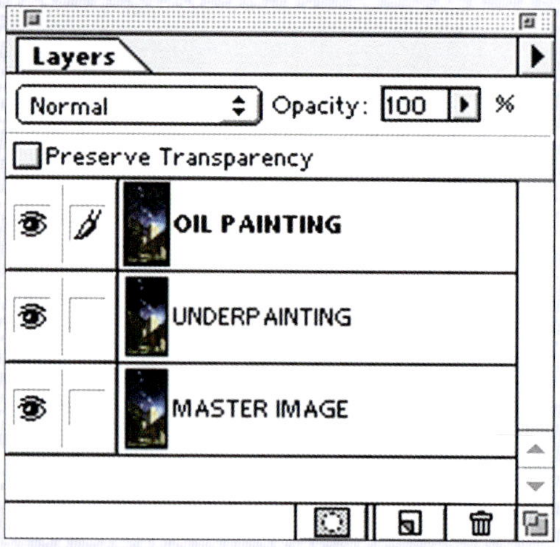

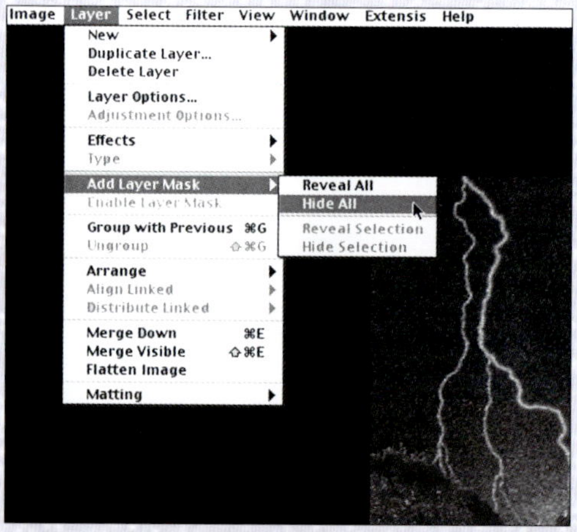

1 A Layer Mask was created with the Reveal/Hide All selection option. This mask is used to apply sections of the uppermost layer on the underlying image.

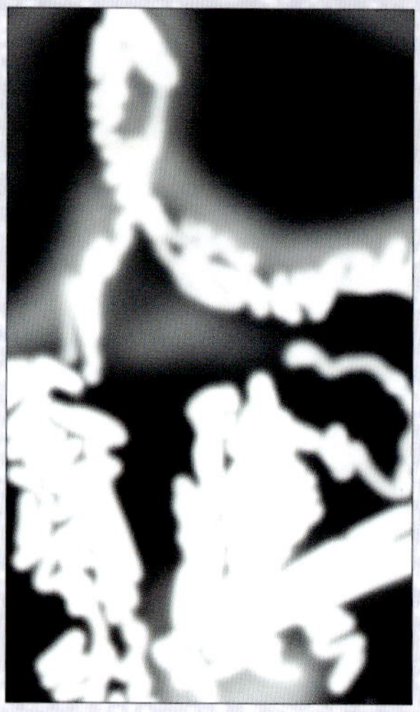

2 This image shows the painted layer mask. White areas are holes in the mask, grey areas allow partial masking and black areas are masked out completely.

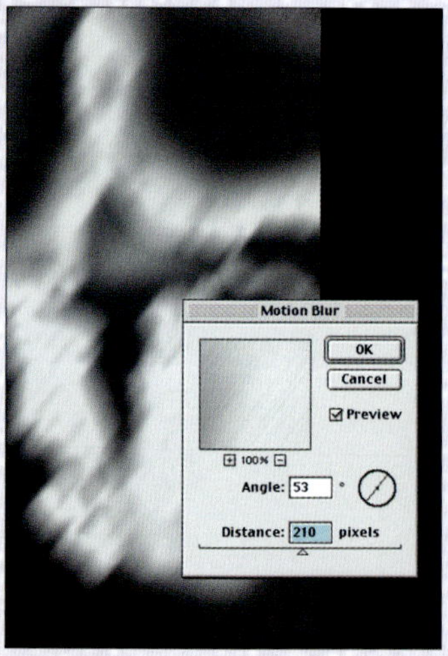

3 The Motion Blur filter was run to soften the image, blurring the transitions between the areas of oil paint and the underpainting.

The finished image unmasked

The deep blue of the stormy sky contrasts sharply with the sunlit churchyard, lending the finished image a surrealist edge

Some areas were overpainted with small brushes, an airbrush, and the Smudge tool to re-establish detail

Areas of light and shade were added using the Dodge and Burn tools

The Unsharp Mask filter was used to lift the contrast and detail slightly

Painter
Photoshop
Plug-ins
Drawing Tablet

Composing a montage

A series of images can be unified by composing them into a montage and painting them using a single technique. Here, three photographs taken in one sitting were selected, so the boy's clothes are the same and the poses work well together. However, this technique is also effective when using images from different sources.

Objective Creating a portrait montage from photographs

Teaching Points

1 Drag and drop layers

2 Unifying images through painting techniques

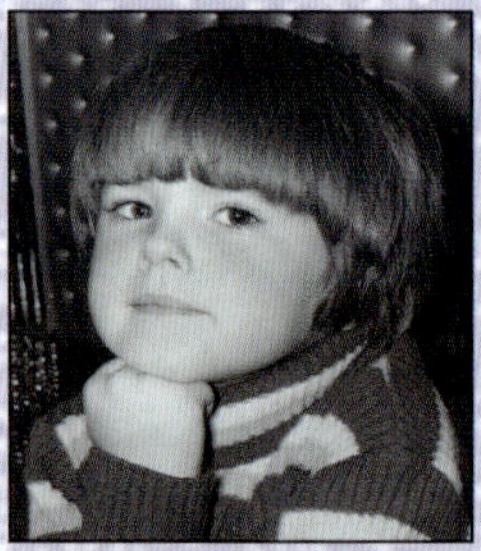

1 A new file was opened at the final printed size and resolution needed for an inkjet print. The main image was dragged onto the new file using Photoshop's Moving tool, creating a new layer above the white paper of the image. The image was sized using the Transform tool and placed centrally in the composition. The same process was used to drag the other two images into position. The backgrounds of the three images were crudely painted out using the Eraser tools. When perfect cutouts are not needed it is quicker to erase background detail with a large brush. Once the composition was in place the layers were flattened to provide a template for the sketch.

2 The image was opened in MetaCreations Painter and a clone made. The Tracing Paper facility and a chalk cloner brush were used to sketch in the portraits. Once the rough sketch was complete the image was saved as a Photoshop document.

3 The sketch was opened in Photoshop and detail added to the faces. The composed image from Step 1 was then sampled using Photoshop's Rubber Stamp tool, which can sample a complete image or a selected area. Brushwork was added to the sketched image using a low opacity brush. The eyes and facial features were painted using this technique. Detail was added using paintbrushes, while the Dodge and Burn tools added shadows and highlights.

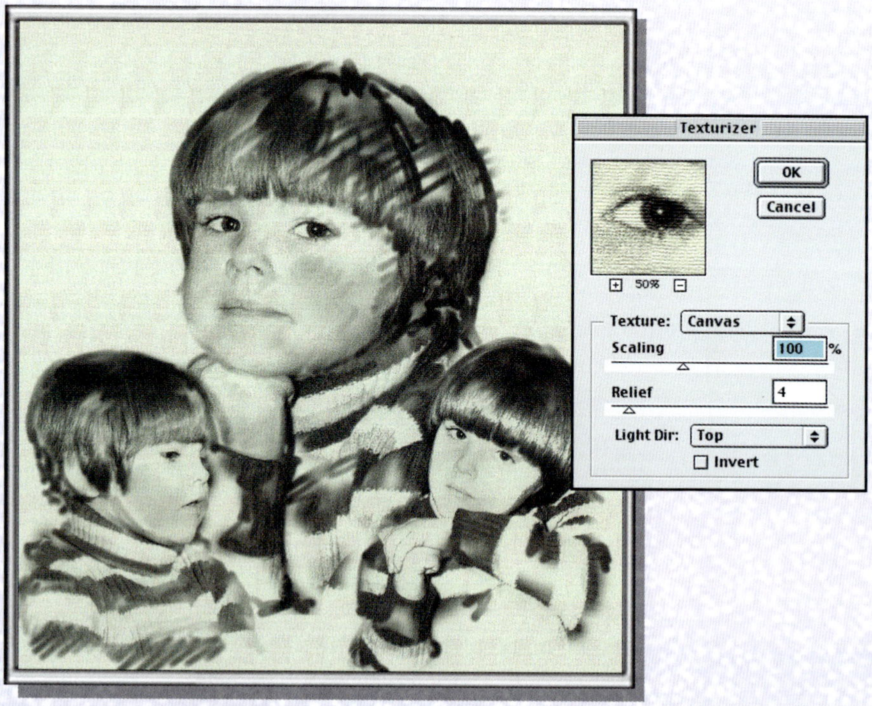

4 A neutral tan paper colour was selected. Mid-tone backgrounds are effective, because they allow the artist to emphasize highlights with pale colours. The cartridge paper effect was enhanced by running Photoshop's Texturizer filter, adjusting the settings to give an overall paper texture.

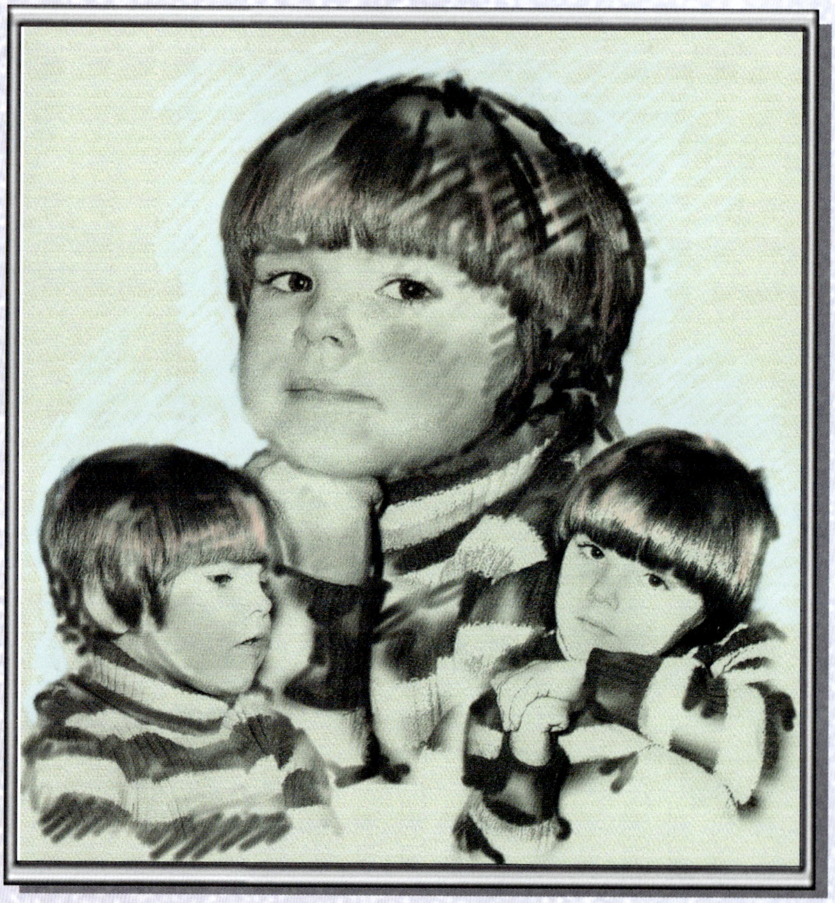

5 The image was opened in Painter, where a range of real media artists' techniques can be replicated. To give the pencil work more interest the tonal work was smudged using a simple water brush, a technique that softened some of the harsh tonal variations. Pale-coloured chalks were used to give the portraits a halo effect and add colour to the highlights in the hair.

The finished portrait montage

The Rubber Stamp tool was used to sample detail from the original photographs. This technique works particularly well around the eyes

Painter's chalk brushes react with the digital paper's key. Light pressure on the stylus increases the amount of paper visible through the marks

Highlights were added to the faces using the Photoshop Dodge tool on a very low setting, focusing on the quarter-tones and highlight areas of the image

The Photoshop Texturizer filter was used to increase the illusion of a watercolour paper substrate. The portrait was then printed out on 125gsm watercolour paper using a desktop 1440dpi inkjet printer. The result is an amazingly realistic chalk and charcoal drawing

Painter

Photoshop

Adobe Paint Daubs

Drawing Tablet

Painting over a traced image

Loosely based on Pierre-Auguste Renoir's peoplescapes, this café scene began life as a photograph, scanned in and cropped to the finished size of the painting. A focal point is created by lifting the foreground subjects from the subtle painting of the background, where colours are lightened and slightly muted.

Objective To paint a street scene in the style of Renoir, creating a focal point for the image

Teaching Points

1 Using Painter's Cloner tools and virtual tracing paper

2 Sketching and blocking in areas of colour

3 Using Photoshop's Layer Blending modes to add detail

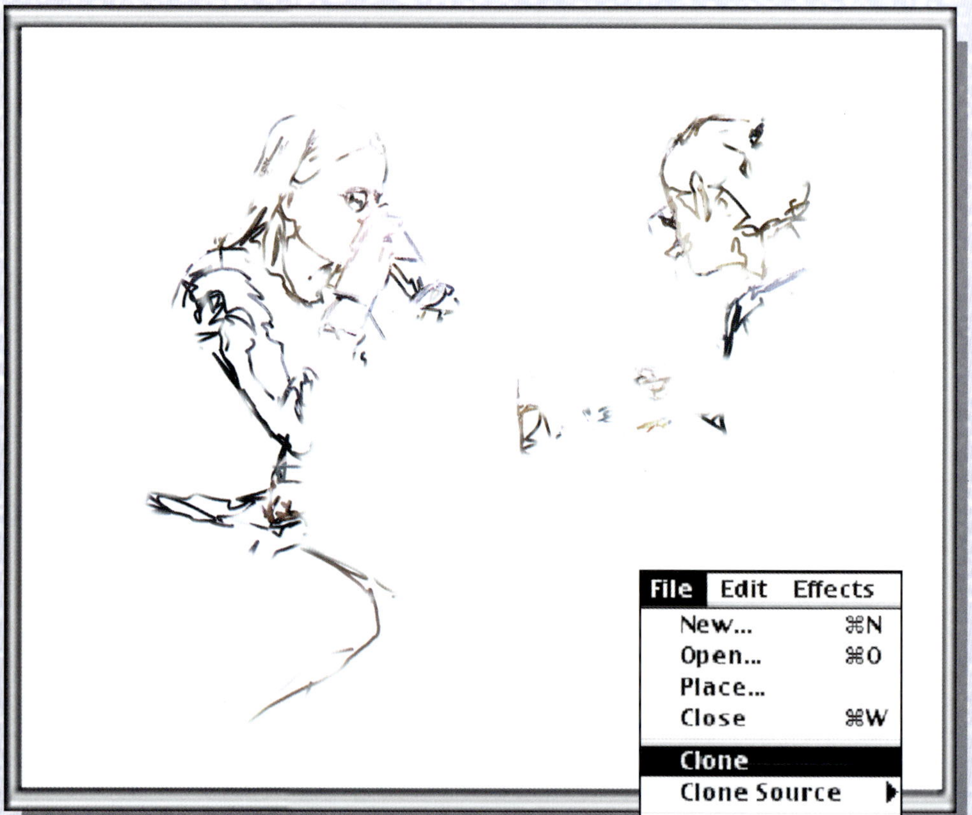

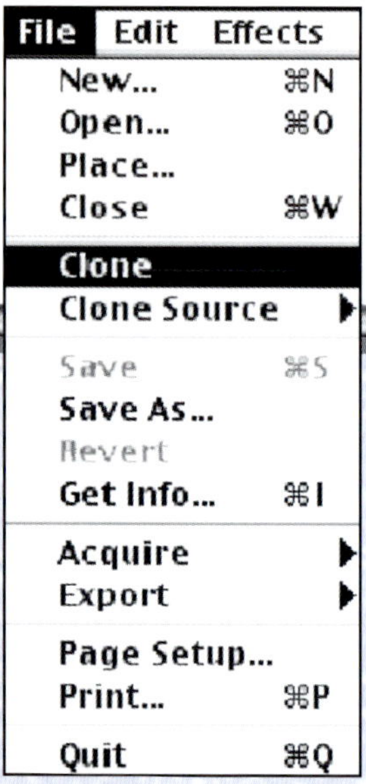

1 The image was opened in MetaCreations Painter and a clone made, creating a copy of the file for the painting. The Cloner Coloured Pencil tool was used to sketch in the main figures using the tracing paper image as a guide. The image is selected and then deleted, giving a blank canvas to work on.

2 The sketch was built up until all the necessary detail had been roughed in. By switching the Tracing Paper mode on and off it is possible to view the sketch over the ghosted image of the original.

3 The Tracing Paper was switched off and an oil cloner brush selected. Colour on the main figures was blocked in over the sketch.

4 Detail in the background was kept soft and loose to focus the eye on the main figures. This created a focal point for the artwork.

5 With the sketch completed the Cloner tools were no longer needed. Detail was added using smaller brushes, being careful to retain the relaxed style of the painting. The contrast between foreground and background had become too strong, so the background was darkened slightly to re-establish balance.

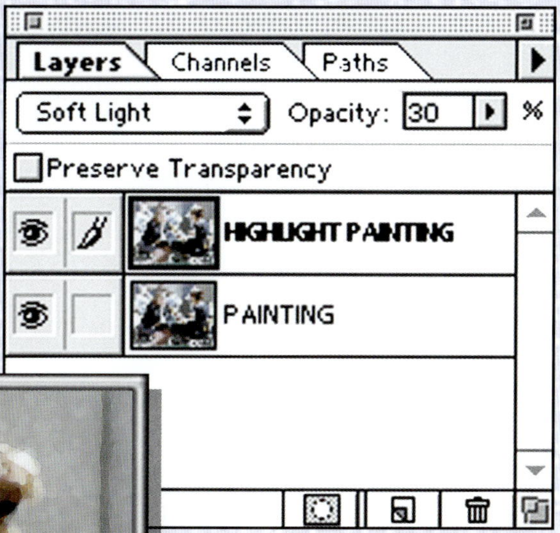

6 The image was layered above the painting and the two blended using Photoshop's Soft Light mode. The opacity of the highlight image was lowered to 30%, giving a more subtle effect.

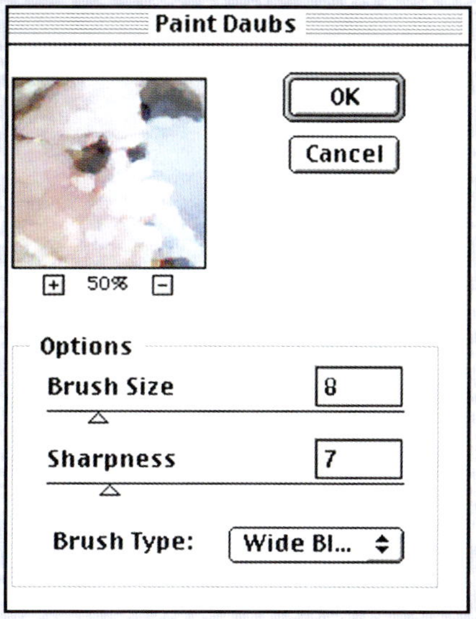

To increase the highlights in the image, a copy was made and the Paint Daubs filter was run. This produced a loose, painterly image with more intense highlights.

The finished café scene

Areas of light and shade were adjusted using Photoshop's Dodge and Burn tool

Photoshop's Hue and Saturation controls were used to slightly desaturate and lighten the background

Painter's Distorto brush was used to carefully move colours around and give the paint viscosity

A white border was added around the image and an airbrush used to soften the transition between the image and the border

Creating a three-dimensional painting

This project was inspired by the work of artist Alfred Wallis. His naive style lends itself to working directly in MetaCreations Painter. The image was created with the mouse, and the crude and uneven line work achieved by drawing with the wrong hand. Wallis would often paint onto found driftwood so, following his lead, this image has been superimposed onto a virtual pebble. Don't be afraid of experimenting with different shaped canvases.

Objective To naively paint an image and apply the painting to a virtual pebble

Teaching Points
1 Drawing directly with Painter
2 Painting in a naive style
3 Transferring the image onto a virtual pebble

1 A new document was created in MetaCreations Painter. The basic outline of the ship was drawn using a 2B pencil and the mouse.

2 A large, loaded oil brush was selected and used to paint the background. The whole background was blocked in before working over the top with shorter, directional brushstrokes in slightly varying colours.

3 The boat and sails are painted in the same way. The colour palette was limited to a few strong shades, with a little black added to slightly dull the vibrant colours.

4 The colour work is held together by crudely outlining the shapes. Painter's Charcoal brushes were selected to outline the boat.

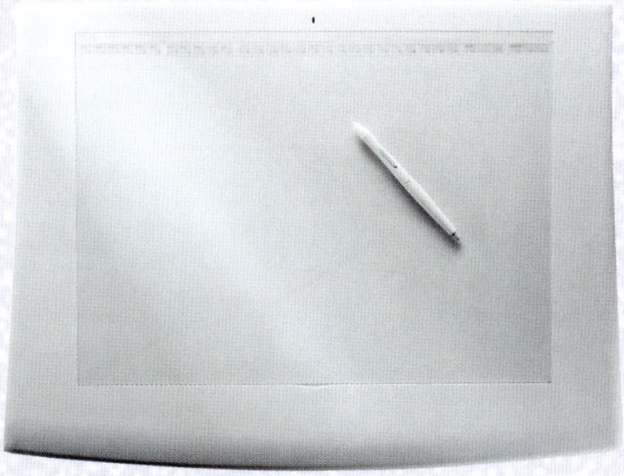

Some tablets have programmable buttons that can be used as shortcuts for repetitive tasks. The buttons can be set to many variables, including opening files, creating a new documents, saving work and closing a document.

5 To add texture and further interest, the Paint Alchemy filter was run on a copy of the painting. This image was merged with the painting on a Low Opacity setting, slightly changing the original. The image was copied to a new layer and the Grain filter in Photoshop applied. This produced the graphic black and white textured image below, which was then blended with the painting.

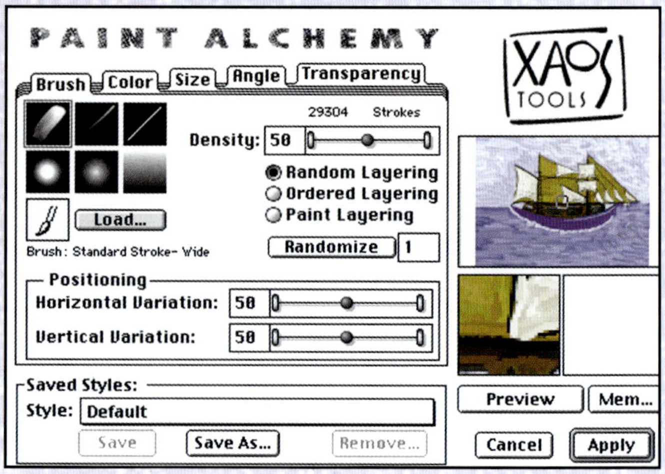

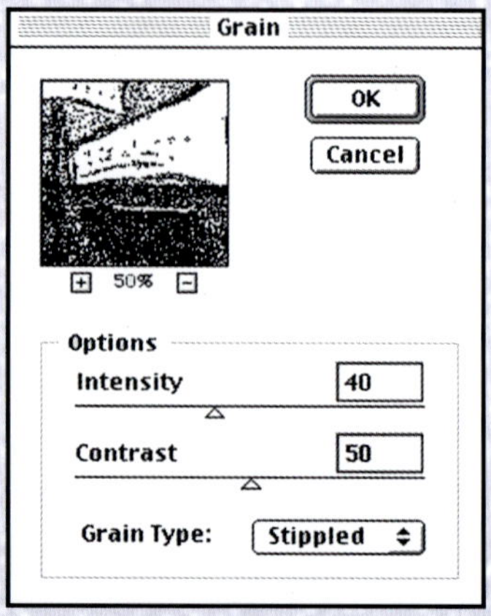

Applying a texture to the image adds interest and helps to replicate real media painting

6 The resulting texture was effective but had become overpowering. To soften the effect, the untextured painting was copied onto the textured version and merged. The opacity was set at 50% to halve the textured effect.

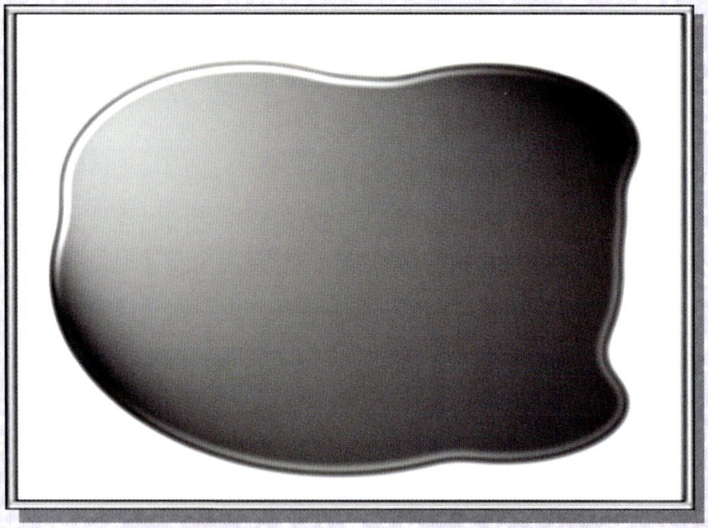

7 To create the shape of the pebble a rough selection was made with the Lasso tool, filling the shape with black. The edges of the pebble were softened by first running a Gaussian Blur filter and then increasing the contrast to bring back a rich black tone. Finally, the direction highlight was added with Photoshop's Lighting Effects filter, aiming a strong spotlight across the pebble.

1 To compose the painting onto the virtual pebble the image was copied to a layer above the pebble shape. A mask was created around the pebble.

2 The Layers Blending mode was changed to allow the highlight and shadows from the pebble to react with the painting. To achieve a convincing three-dimensional painting the mode was change to Hard Light and the opacity reduced slightly.

The finished pebble painting

Photoshop's Blending and Opacity controls allow the form of the pebble to act upon the flat 2-D painting

To finish the image off the pebble was placed onto some virtual sand. A new layer was created and filled with a flat, sandy colour. Running the Add Noise filter at a high setting added the grain. Areas were selected with the Lasso tool and darkened slightly by adjusting the Brightness controls and the streaks were produced by running the Motion Blur filter at a very high setting. Photoshop's powerful Wave distortion filter gave a realistic pattern to the sand

A slight drop shadow was added below the pebble to make it look as if it is sitting on the sand

Photoshop

Plug-in

Creating texture and lighting effects

While digital artwork has many advantages over real media, there is a danger that flat colour work and smooth gradations can look too uniform to convey any energy. The digital artist can, however, add texture at any stage of the painting. Tools are available to add canvas and paper textures, or light the surface of the electronic paper. Using textures in your work can add an extra dimension, and liven up flat imagery.

Objective To paint a figure study using filters to create textures

Teaching Points

1 Tracing from a scanned pencil sketch
2 Laying flat colours
3 Using filters for texture
4 Dramatic effects with blending modes

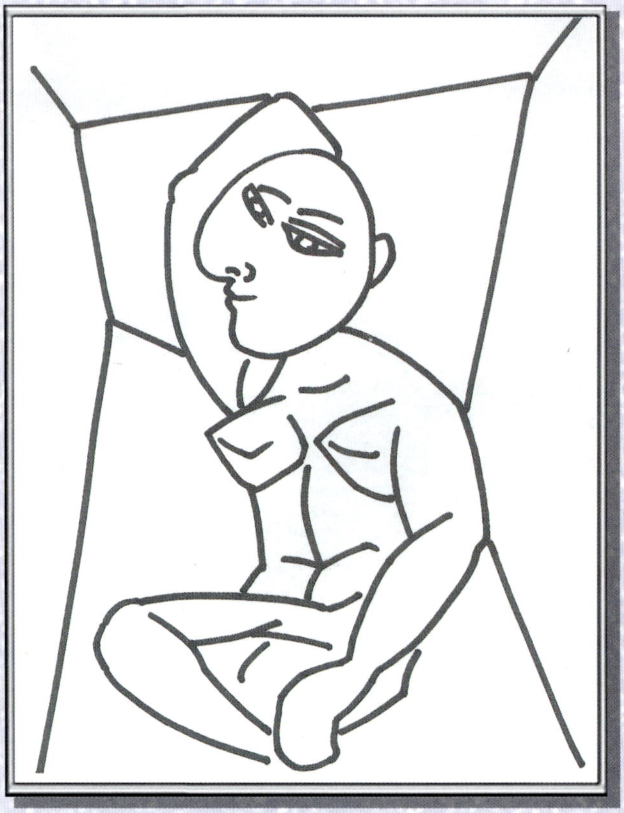

1 The image was first sketched on paper to establish the composition. The size of the finished image was determined and the sketch scanned to the correct size and resolution.

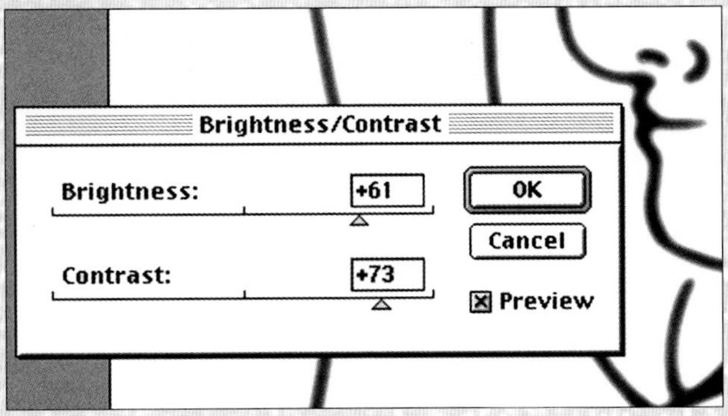

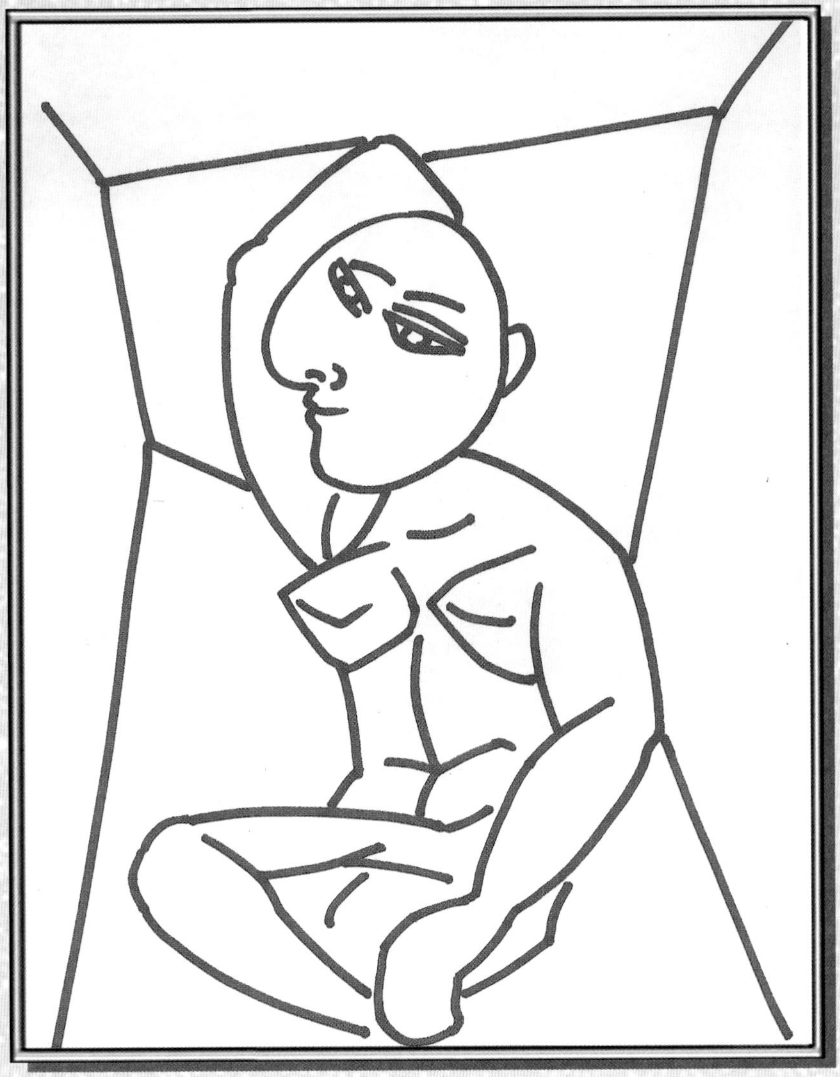

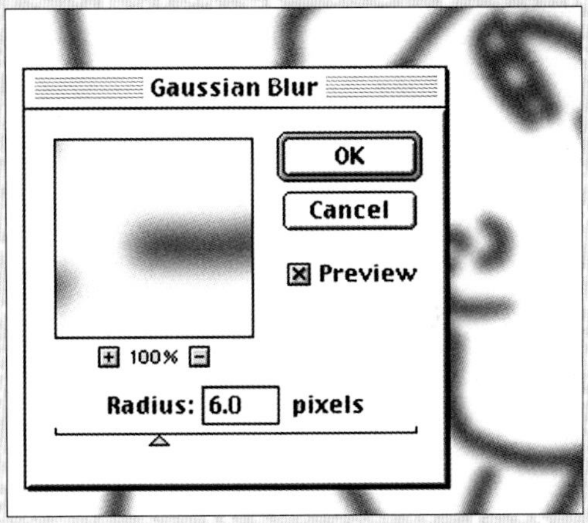

2 The sketch was traced over using a broad, flat brush and black paint. To give the line work a painterly feel, the Gaussian Blur filter was run at a very low setting. This softens the line work, losing any harsh edges or corners. With the softened sketch opened, the Brightness and Contrast controls were adjusted. Setting the Contrast high makes the line black again but with a smooth, soft edge. Adjusting the Brightness alters the weight of the line; this technique gives realistic brush-type line work, where the weight varies slightly along the line's length.

3 Three layers were created to hold the image. Layer one contained the completed tracing, layer two would hold colour for the image's background and layer three contained the foreground figure. Areas of the image were selected with the Lasso tool, and filled by selecting a colour and pressing Delete or Option Delete. The background was blocked in using a limited colour palette.

4 Once the flat colour was in place, the Add Noise filter was run to add colour and grain to the flat colour work. The Adobe Texturizer filter was run to add a canvas texture to the selection.

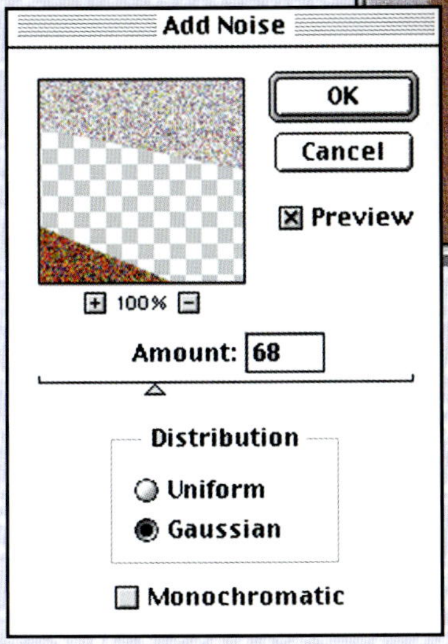

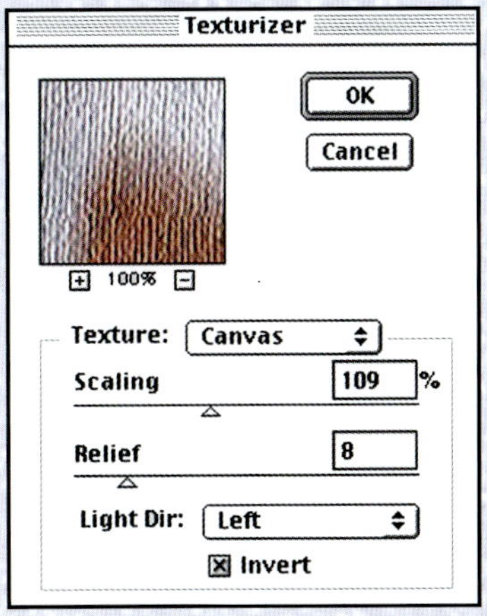

The Adobe Texturizer filter is used to add a surface texture to the artwork. The variables include different preset textures of Canvas, Sandstone and Burlap which can vary in size and depth.

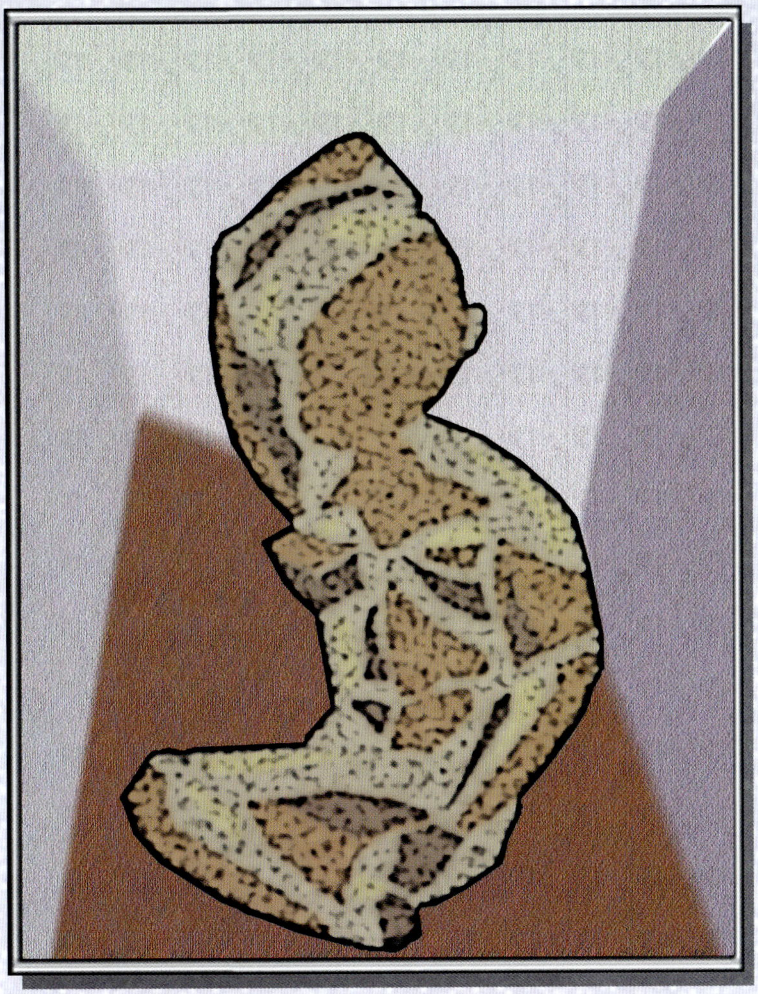

5 The same process was used to texturize the figure. Different amounts of Noise and varying settings were applied to the Texture filter.

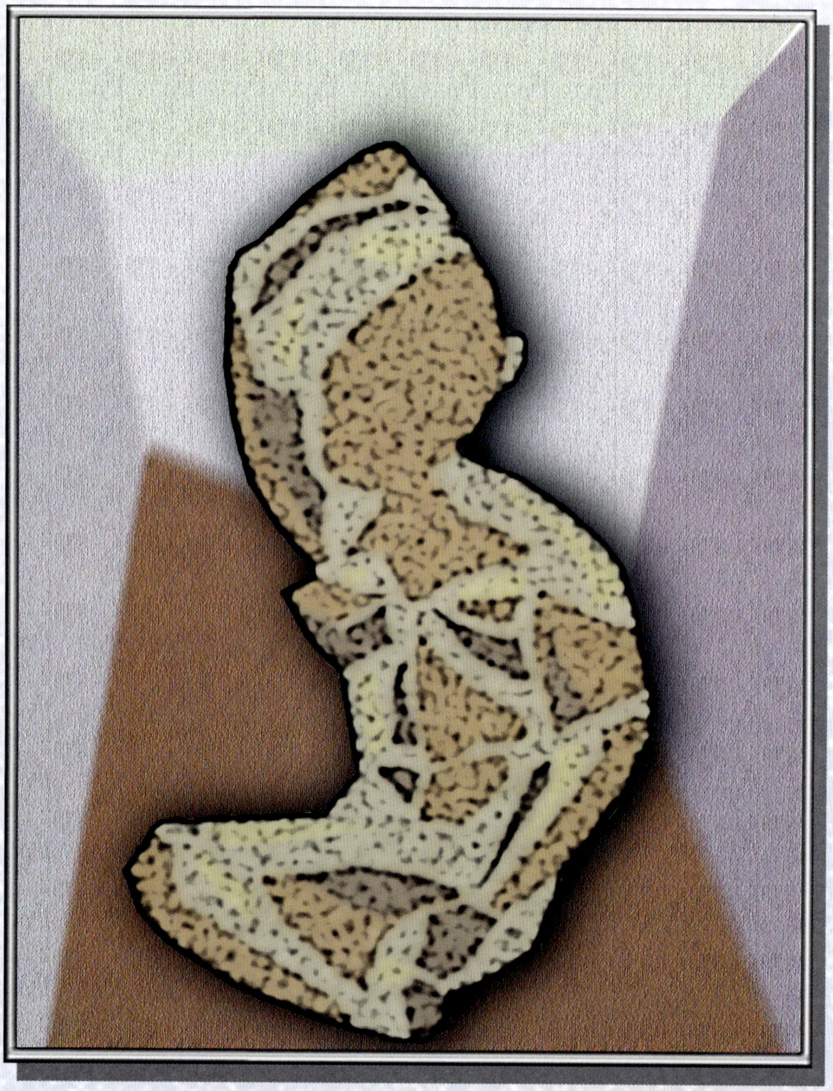

6 Depth can be created in an image with the use of lighting effects. Here, a drop shadow and carefully placed highlight help to lead the eye towards the focal point of the image.

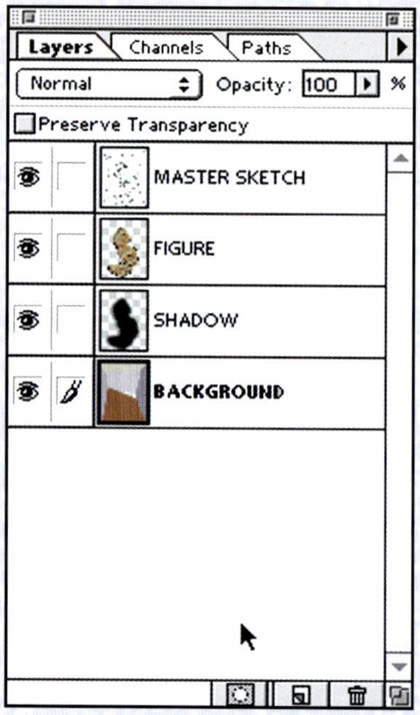

1 To lift the figure slightly from the background a soft drop shadow was created. Using the figure as a mask, a new layer was made and filled with black. This was softened with the Gaussian Blur filter and moved so that it lay slightly below and to the right of the figure.

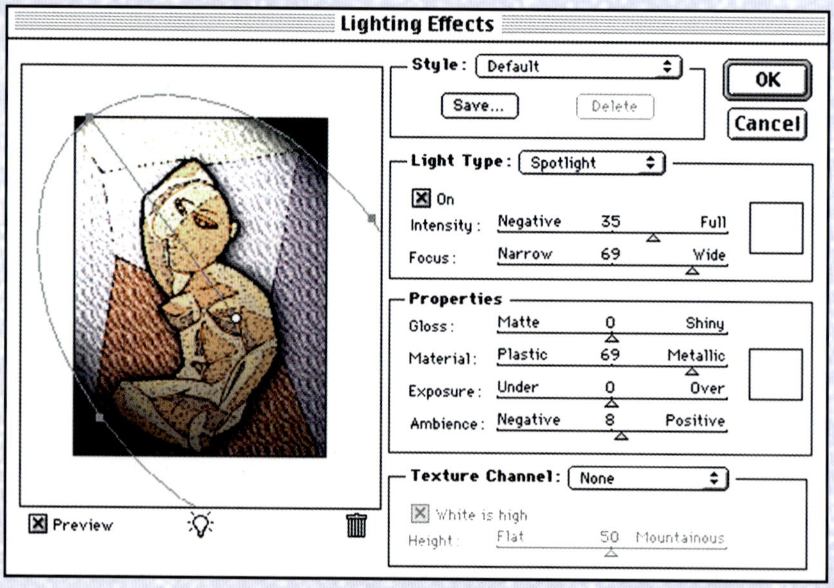

2 With the image flattened, the Lighting Effects filter was run to highlight the centre. Further texture can be added to the image by selecting a texture channel and adjusting the Mountainous slider. For the finished image the Lighting Effects filter was softened with Photoshop's Fade command. Adjusting the Fade Opacity returns proportionately to the unfiltered image.

The finished nude study

Running the Lighting Effects filter over the image unified the foreground and background

The original tracing was copied to a layer above the painting and the Blending mode adjusted to Multiply. This darkened the sketched outline, giving the final image bold lines

The emphasis of this image lies with drawing and form. The colour palette was deliberately limited to prevent it detracting from the line work

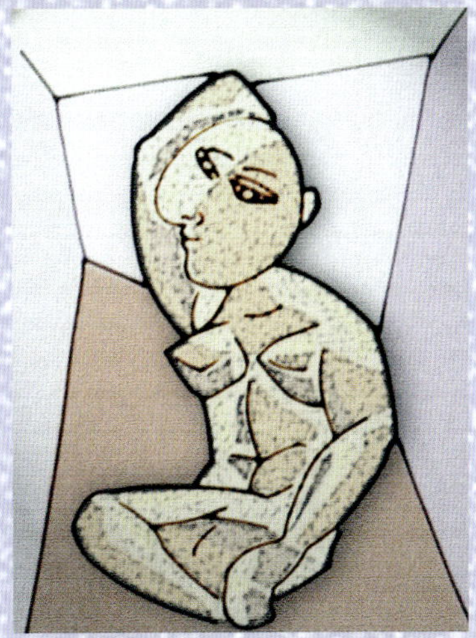

The layered image
These two images show how dramatic changes can be made to the artwork by simply changing the Blending mode between the tracing layer and the underlying coloured artwork.

Photoshop

Plug-in

Distorting images for abstract effects

This project involves experimenting with an image's colour and texture to form the basis for an abstract image. Newcomers to digital art may view the Distortion filters as being too quirky to be of any practical use. However, there are many creative uses for these filters. Here, they are used to distort images while retaining the subject's colour, an invaluable tool for creating montage and abstract work.

Objective Developing a familiar image into an abstract composition

Teaching Points

1 Using Distortion filters to create shapes
2 Using an image for its colour and texture

1 After scanning an image of a flower it was cropped to a square format. Holding the Shift key while using the Marquee tool will constrain its proportions to a square. Once the area is selected use the Crop command to trim excess image data away.

2 Half the image area was selected, again using the Marquee tool and then inverting the image (Image⟶Adjust⟶ Invert or Command I on the keyboard). Experimenting with image inversions can reveal interesting colourways, as the computer's colour wheel will create shades that the traditional real media artist may not be familiar with.

3 The Polar Coordinates Distortion filter was run to bend the image into a circular shape.

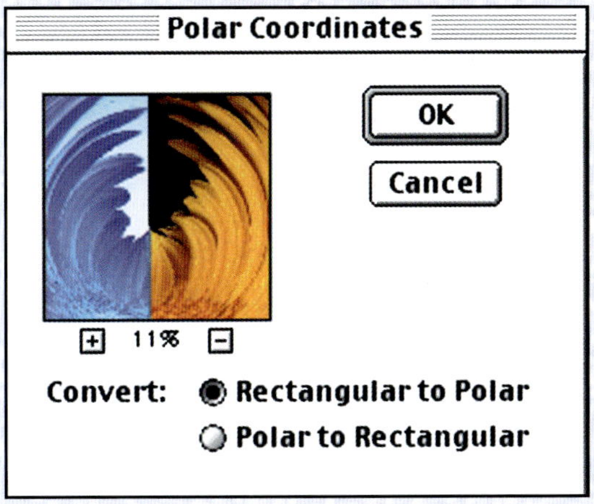

4 The Twirl distortion filter was run, twisting the image around its centre point by 243°. Running this filter several times with lower settings will produce the same distortion, while retaining more of the data from the original image. Using the filter once at this larger setting will lose much of the original's detail. An interesting distortion can be achieved by running the filter in a clockwise direction, and then running it again anti-clockwise at the same angle.

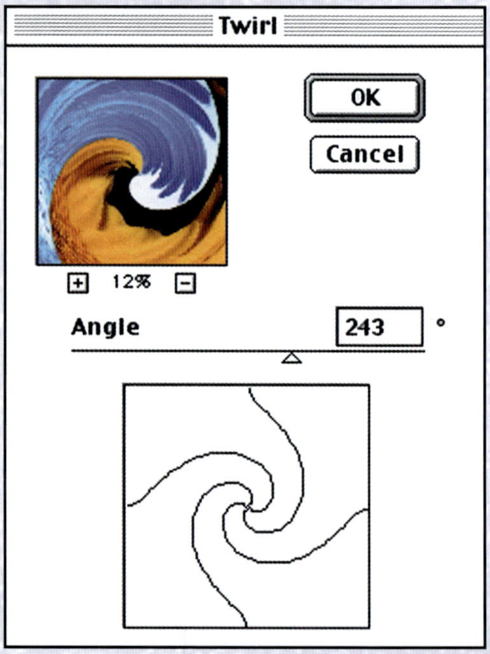

5 Xenofex Shower Door filter was used to give the image a more painterly feeling. Although the filter appears to have little practical application, it can give very realistic painterly brush strokes and can be useful to the digital artist who is not using a stylus.

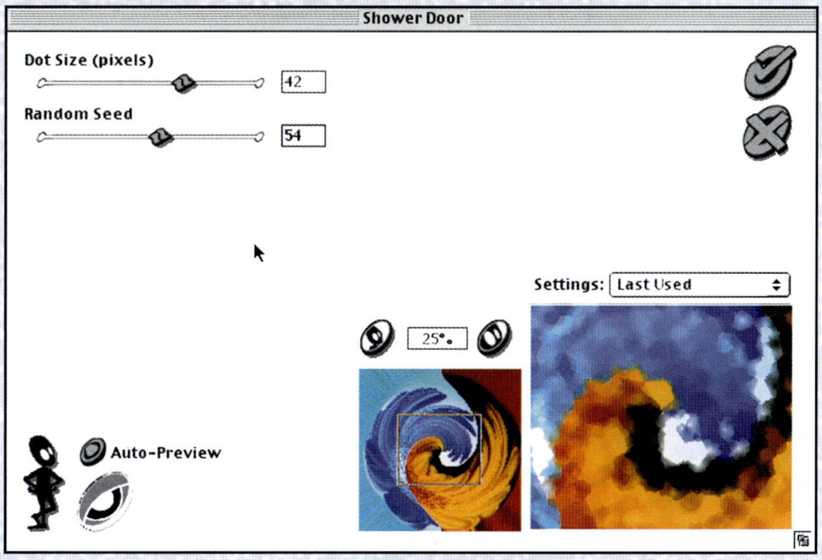

6 To finish off the image the ZigZag distortion filter was run. This created a pond ripple around the image's centre. The ZigZag filter replicates a ripple effect, with variables including the number of waves, and whether the distortion radiates out or spirals from the centre of an image.

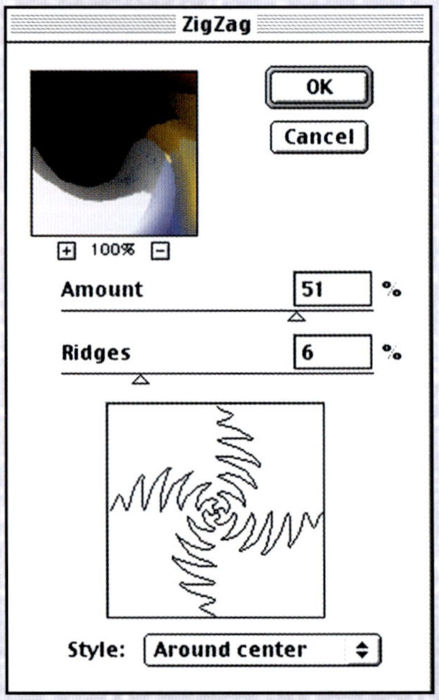

The finished abstract

The image was lifted from the background by applying a drop shadow. Photoshop's Layer Effects menu can add automatic drop shadows to layers, with variable parameters including Colour, Transparency, Blur and Blending mode

The images were grouped together with strong coloured boxes as linking elements, using the primary printing ink colours of cyan, magenta, yellow, and black

The final composition was made by creating 11 images from the original flower image. The Distortion filters were used, experimenting with the colours using the Hue and Saturation controls

Getting Technical

Saving artwork: file formats

It can be daunting saving artwork when faced with a dialogue box with several options for file formats. Consider where the final image will be printed, whether the image will have to be re-edited and how you intend to archive the finished work.

FILE FORMATS

This is a brief look at some of the possible file formats available and their potential uses. The final decision will be dependent upon each user's own way of working but a little knowledge of the main formats will influence which format to choose.

Photoshop

This is the native file format of Adobe Photoshop. It will allow you to save any elements that are native to Photoshop, such as layers, clipping paths, channels and Photoshop effects, which will not translate to other image editing software. The advantage of saving in this format is that it is easy to edit and manipulate the image.

BMP

An often-used format for the Windows platform, BMP allows the artist to save 24-bit images with loss-less compression (no loss of image data). This format is often used to create Wallpaper for computer desktops.

Compuserve GIF

A format aimed at web design, GIF only allows images to be saved with 256 colours, equating to index colour mode. When saving to this format it is good practice to first make a copy of the original artwork, as images converted to Index colour can look very different and are often disappointing.

EPS

The Encapsulated PostScript file format is very useful when an image has to be exported to another program, image editor or page make-up software. Any images that have embedded clipping paths, for example, should be saved as an EPS. Another advantage is that Postscript is the language used by laser printers, so there will be fewer printer errors when printing from a file saved in the same language. Also, the files can be sent to PostScript printers without needing any software, as printing information is encapsulated within the file. This can be useful when sending to a bureau for output. One last consideration is that the file size will increase by approximately 25%, as this extra information is stored with the image.

DCS

Desktop Colour Separation files split the image into its compound parts of cyan, magenta, yellow, black and placement/preview. The advantages of this system become apparent when sending a large file to print at an image bureau. An 80MB file would have to be sent to print for each of the four-colour separations, while sending a DCS file would enable the bureau to output four separate 20MB files, greatly reducing print time and cost.

Filmstrip

This file format is used for video and animation work.

JPEG

Developed by the Joint Photographic Expert Group, this file format is used to save an image at a greatly reduced file size. It offers excellent compression, although care has to be taken when deciding how much compression is applied to an image: too much and the data loss can be noticeable, with the image losing colours or abnormal pixelation occuring. Files can be compressed from a megabyte to 100 kilobytes without losing image quality, making this format ideal for sending files over the Internet or by e-mail.

PCX

This format has been superseded by BMP and was used in the early days of DOS and PC Paintbrush.

PICT

The PICT file format is native to the Macintosh platform and is most often used for low resolution screen grabs.

TIFF

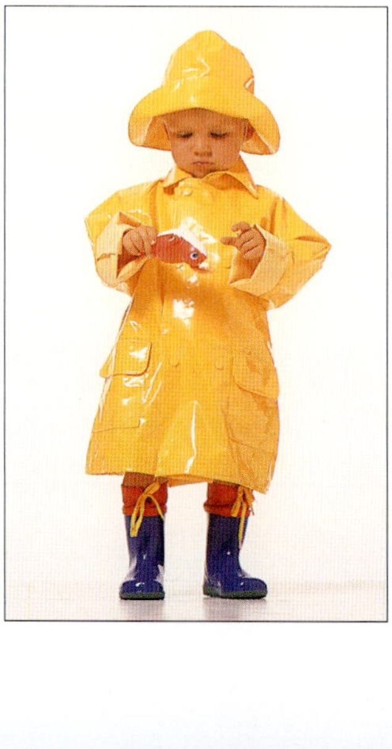

EPS

TIFF

Tagged Image File Format is one of the most popular formats used by both Macintosh and Windows users. When saving, most paint and editing software will offer compression facilities which reduce file size without loss of image quality. TIFF is the format most used in the design field and is probably, after native file formats, the most useful way of saving your work.

RIFF

The Raster Image File Format is the native file format for MetaCreations Painter. Saving work in this format will preserve wet layers and image data that can only be read within Painter.

WHICH SHOULD I USE?

The file format you choose will depend on the final destination of your image. While the image is in creation, using the native file formats will preserve any material that may need to be re-edited. At a later stage your work can be saved in a format suitable for its destination. If the image is to be used on the Internet, save it accordingly.

Black and white images

The TIFF format is suitable for most black and white printing, and offers the best compatibility range.

Colour images

Printing colour images requires the image to be saved with all the image data relating to resolution and bit depth. The best formats for printing colour images are TIFF and EPS. Ask your service bureau for their preferred format before sending work to be printed.

Printing to desktop inkjet printers

Again, TIFF format offers the widest compatibility range. Do not use the EPS file, as most desktop inkjets are not PostScript and image quality will be lost. This will often result in greatly distorted images or rather unusual colours.

Saving for the web

The two choices are GIF and JPEG. Both offer file compression and 256 Index colour, compatible with web browsing software. JPEG, however, has the advantage of greater image quality.

Archiving

The choice when archiving depends on a number of factors. These include considering file compression to reduce disk space, whether archiving to hard disk or removable media, the importance of image quality and if the file is to be archived within its native file format. JPEG images can be very small and use less disk space. TIFF files keep image quality intact while compressing the file size. Painter's RIFF or Photoshop files should be saved when it is essential to store image data such as wet layers, effects or channels and clipping paths.

JPEG

PICT

GIF

Professional digital output

At some stage in the creative process the digital painter will want to 'realize' the artwork by outputting to a print. Some desktop colour inkjet printers are capable of professional printing without the usual expense, although professional print quality will always produce preferable quality, colour and permanency. If you decide to print out through a professional printing bureau it is good practice to find out the available options and techniques, and the technical questions affecting colour conversion. Most good bureaux will be able to advise you how to set up your digital files to their preferred method.

Colour conversion

Most output devices will require your digital files to be supplied as CMYK files rather than RGB. Care has to be taken when converting your files that any RGB colours you have used that are out of CMYK's gamut are converted to printable colours. Photoshop has a range of tools that will warn you of any colours that will be lost in the conversion process. These can then be changed to printable colours before conversion. Some output bureaux will accept RGB files and then convert to CMYK for you by creating special custom colour tables in Photoshop.

Iris printing

One of the most common art printing techniques, an Iris print uses inkjet technology. Water-soluble vegetable-based CMYK dyes are sprayed onto paper through very fine nozzles. The receiver paper is wrapped around a rotating drum and the fine ink droplets are sprayed on at millions of droplets per second. Watercolour paper and heavier substrates can be used to give the finished print a textured base. There is no visible dot pattern on the print, making it ideal for fine art output.

Dye sublimation

Dye sublimation works on a similar process as the Iris print and produces a glossy, continuous tone print. Dye subs tend to be used by designers to check work before normal four-colour printing. Their main disadvantage is that they are susceptible to damage through humidity, with the surface being easily smudged. Accurate colour matching is far harder than with Iris.

Pictography

Direct photographic printing from your digital file, a pictography print offers the same bright luminous colours as the dye-sub but has improved registration and permanency. The digital image is lasered onto a donor sheet, which is then printed onto photographic paper. Ultraviolet inhibitors can be coated onto the print to extend the colour's life.

Bureau Output
A good operator will be able to adjust the printer settings and it is always worth marking important areas with a written note, or talking to the operator about what can be achieved.
A bureau that maintains its printers well will also make a difference to the quality of the finished image.

ORIGINAL

Transparencies

Digital files can be printed to transparent media, primarily using photographic transparent films from 35mm up to and beyond 10 x 8 in (25 x 20cm). A film recorder uses laser technology to write RGB data onto ordinary photographic film, which is then processed in the normal way. Talk to your bureau about how to save your files, as resolution and bit depth are different in transparent output when compared to other output mediums.

IRIS

Delicate colour that represents a 10% dot or less will not print and images should be saved slightly darker than normal. High contrast can also mean a loss of detail in the darker areas. Fine lines may also suffer quality loss. The texture below is due to the use of a heavier type of paper. Canvas can also be used and overpainted.

DYE SUBLIMATION

The colours will be slightly warmer than the original and the print glossy and smooth but there will be a slight dot texture to the image. Fine lines and text will suffer quality loss.

INKJET

The quality of an inkjet print at a bureau can be very different to that achieved at home but a dot and a grainy texture will still be visible. The colours will also be more saturated than the original image.

Permanency of your prints

A primary concern when printing is the permanency of the finished print. Most inkjet printing inks will fade when exposed to ultraviolet light; these inks are known as fugitive. A protective coating can be applied by silkscreen to help prevent colours fading, or a UV varnish can be sprayed over the finished print. Take care to use a spray varnish that is alcohol-based, as printing inks are water-soluble and the image could run. If possible, test the spray on a spare print.

Getting to know a printer

The final step in producing good quality prints from your digital artwork is to experiment with different models of printer. A piece of artwork will look dramatically different when outputted on different printers. Creating colour tables for specific printers will help you to judge what works best on a particular model. Talking to your bureau will reveal colour settings and ways of working that will suit your style of painting.

One last point: 'happy' mistakes can and will happen when printing work. Don't be afraid to exploit them.

Glossary

Alla prima Direct painting without first sketching

Anti-aliasing Softening the edges between strong tonal changes within an image. Smooths out jagged edges sometimes created by imaging software

Archive Long term storage of digital files

Bit depth The amount of colour information contained within a digital image

Bitmap An image made up of individual pixels or tiles

Blur Softening an image, making it appear out of focus

Brightness The overall tonal value, light or darkness of an image

Broken colour Using rough dabs of colour with paper show-through and allowing the viewer to optically mix the colours

Brushes Types of computer paintbrushes and pencils available to the digital artist

Brushing Using the brushstrokes to effect in painting

Canvas The blank space the computer creates for the digital artist to paint on

CCD Charged coupled device. The computer chip in a scanning device that converts light into image data

CD-ROM Compact disk containing computer data, read only memory. Data can be read from the disk but not written on to it

Channels Greyscale components of a multichannel document. Each channel could represent RGB channel information

Clip art Ready-made artwork that can be used free of any royalties

Clone Making a copy of an image to use as a virtual tracing paper

CMYK colour The standard primary ink colours for four-colour printing: cyan, magenta, yellow and key (black)

Collage Using analogous elements within an artwork

Colour matching System of matching colours viewed on screen and in print

Colour modes The bit depth of the image, i.e. Bitmap, greyscale, index, RGB, CMYK

Complementary colours Colours opposite each other on a colour wheel

Compression A way of making digital files smaller to use less disk space

Contrast Two areas in an image with greatly different tonal values

CPU Computer Processing Unit. The part of the computer that performs the digital commands

Craquelure Distressed surface texture

Crosshatching Building tones by drawing fine lines across each other

DAT Digital audio tape. Used to back-up and store digital files

Digital camera An input device that works as a normal camera but captures the image as digital data rather than on conventional film

BROKEN COLOUR

CROSSHATCHING

CRAQUELURE

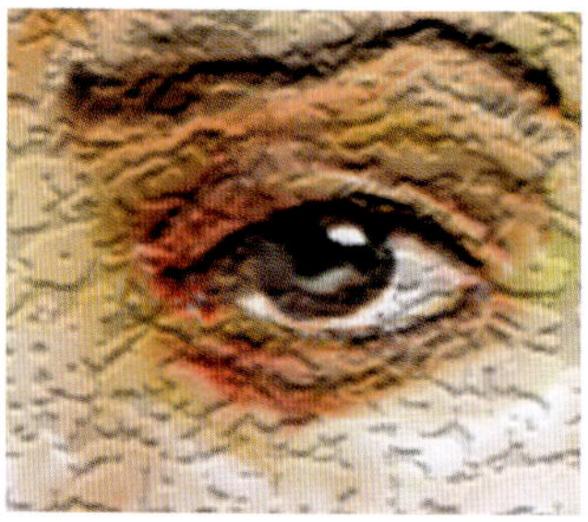

GRADATION

Display The computer's monitor or screen

Dot-gain The amount the printed image's inks will spread on different receiver papers

dpi Dots per inch. Standard measurement of printable information contained in a digital image

Dry brush Painting technique using very little paint, allowing the surface texture to show through

Duotone Printed image made by printing two coloured inks

DVD Digital versatile disk. A new format that can hold vast amounts of data on a disk the same size as a compact disk

Dye sublimation Printing process using water-based inks and shiny photographic quality paper

Feather Softening a selection's edges or smoothly blending areas with tonal contrast

File formats The way the digital file has been saved to computer disk

Filters Plug-ins that work within a host software to create special effects or help production

Firewire High speed peripheral interface, used mainly with digital video

Flatten Flattening a multilayered document

Fractals Natural patterns created by mathematical algorithms

FTP FETCH. The software used to upload and download files from the Internet

Gamut The area of the spectrum that can be seen by different colour modes. RGB colour gamut is larger than CMYK, making it possible to paint with unprintable colours

GIF A file format that only contains index colour information. Suitable for web graphics

Glazing Laying translucent colours over painting to build tone, light and colour

Gradation Smoothly blending two colours over a distance

Gradient Smooth blending between two or more colours

Halftone System used in conventional printing to print shades of a colour using a dot screen

Hard disk The computer's main storage space, can be internal or external

Hardware Any piece of computer machinery, from the computer to the mouse

Hexachrome Six-colour printing process using standard four-colour inks plus blue and red

HSB Hue, saturation, brightness. The three components of individual colour pixel information

Hue The name given to any particular colour, such as red, green, blue

Inkjet Printers that squirt the printing ink through small nozzles or jets onto the receiver paper

Input device Any piece of computer hardware used to input digital information into the computer

Interpolation Image data created by imaging software when an action has occurred. For example, adding in colours when an image has been blurred

Inverting Reversing the image data's tone and colour to give a negative image

Iris Very high resolution inkjet printing system

JPEG Variable, near loss-less, compression file format created by the Joint Photographic Expert Group

Lasso Tools used for freehand selections

Levels Adjustable controls of an image's overall tonal content. Used for increasing or decreasing contrast

Lighting effects A range of filters that create the appearance of lighting the artwork

Line art Bit depth of an image created using only black and white with no greyscale information

lpi Lines per inch, standard measurement system for conventional printing technologies

Mask Digital tool used to mask off or protect areas of the painting

MB Megabyte. Unit of size of digital files

Mixed media Combining different painting or drawing media

Monitor The computer screen. The user's interface with the digital canvas

Mouse Input device used with computers

Negative Inverting an image giving opposite tonal and colour values

Opacity The transparency of an image, usually measured as a percentage of the opaque image

Output devices Any piece of hardware that will output screen or printed digital images

Palettes Parts of a computer programs' interface that contain tools used within the software

Photomontage Making a collage using photographs as base materials

Pixel Picture element, the smallest building block of a digital image

Pixelation Noticeable grain or jagged edges on artwork, usually undesirable

Platform The type of computer system you are using, i.e. PC or Macintosh

Plug-in A small program used within a host program to help production or create special effects

Pointillism Using spots of colour to build up areas of tone within painting

PostScript Adobe's printing language. Used when sending a digital file to a PostScript output device

ppi Pixels per inch, standard measurement of an image's screen resolution

Pressure sensitive Ability to change a tool's output by applying more pressure to the stylus

Rainbow Type of dye sublimation print

RAM Random access memory. Type of computer memory that carries out the bulk of the live work

Rasterize To convert image into pixel information

Removable media Storage devices that can be removed from the computer and hold digital information

Resolution The amount of image data contained in a digital file, usually measured in dpi or ppi

RGB colour The computer's screen primary colours, red, green and blue

RIP Raster image processor. Computer used to print high resolution images

Saturation The purity of colour, or the amount of grey in any given colour. Saturation ranges from pure colour to grey

Save Command for saving digital files to computer disk

Scanner Device for converting photographs (transparencies and prints) into digital information for use in computers

Scratch disk Computer hard disk used by imaging software to run commands outside of RAM memory capabilities

Screen grab Making a copy of the current contents of the monitor

Selection An area of an image than has been masked

Snapshot Temporary capture of screen image

Software Computer programs

Stippling Pattern making and tone building using a stippling or spotting technique

Storage Hardware used to back-up or store digital files

Stylus Pen-like input device used with a tablet for drawing and painting on computer

POINTILLISM

Substrate Paper or receiver for printing, i.e. watercolour paper or canvas

Surface texture Rendering the appearance of a textured surface on an artwork such as canvas

Tablet Base or artboard used with stylus for drawing on computer

Texture Computer simulation of real media textured papers such as watercolour paper

TIFF Tagged Image File Format. The most common file format for digital artwork, useful when importing images into other software

Tiling A memory-saving way of showing and updating a digital image on screen

Toning Overall colour correction using a transparent wash of colour

Underpainting Rough blocked in painting used as a colour sketch beneath final painting

Value Used in conjunction with hue and saturation, value is the name given to the brightness of the image

Video capture Grabbing still images from video devices

Virtual memory Computer system of using hard disk space as extra RAM

Wash Laying a translucent area of watercolour

Wet-in-wet Using wet paint on a wet surface to allow colour to blend softly

Window The area that the digital information is viewed in within the monitor area

STIPPLING

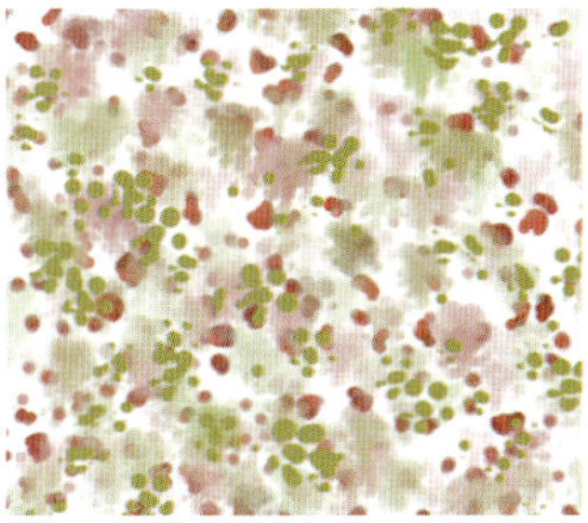

WET-IN-WET

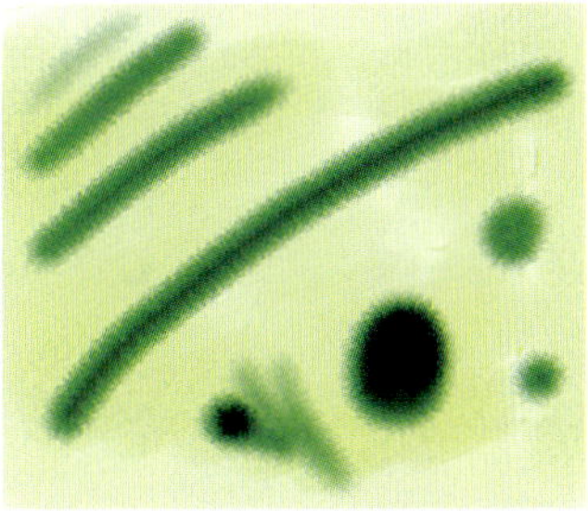

Software Suppliers

Adobe Systems
1585 Charlston Road
PO Box 7900
Mountain View
CA 94039-7900, USA
Tel: (001)-800-833-6687
www.adobe.com

Alien Skin Software
2522 Clark Avenue
Raleigh
NC 27607, USA
Tel: (001) 919-832-4124
www.alienskin.com

Andromeda Software
699 Hampshire Road
Suite 109
Westlake Village
CA 91361, USA
Tel: (001) 805-379-4109
www.andromeda.com

Corel Corporation
1600 Carling Avenue
Ottawa
Ontario K1Z 8R7
Canada
Tel: (001) 613-728-8200
www.corel.com

MetaCreations
6303 Carpinteria Avenue
Carpinteria
CA 93013, USA
Tel: (001) 805-566-6200
www.metacreations.com

Macromedia
600 Townsend Street
Suite 310-W
San Francisco
CA 94103, USA
Tel: (001)-800-898-3762
www.macromedia.com

Xaos Tools
300 Montgomery, 3rd Floor
San Francisco
CA 94104, USA
Tel: (001) 415-487-7000
www.xaostools.com

Index

Acknowledgments

Quarto would like to thank the following for the use of their artwork in the What is Digital Artwork? section:
Katie Hayden, Donald Gambino, Philip Nicholson, Ken Ramey, Brian Wilkins, Paul Crockwell, Randy Sowash, Kit Monroe, Lesley Wilkins, Maureen Nappi, Wendy Grossman.

Quarto Publishing would also like to thank the following hardware manufacturers for their helpful response to requests for information, checking our facts and use of photographs:
Agfa (UK) Ltd, Apple Computer Inc., Canon (UK) Ltd, Compaq (UK), Epsom (UK) Ltd, Iomega Corporation, Logitech S.A., Panasonic (UK), Polaroid (UK) Ltd, Wacom Computer Systems Gmbh and the Customer Helplines of many more.

Thanks also to Clinch/Clarke for their photography.

All other photographs are the copyright of Quarto Publishing plc.

While every effort has been made to contact all copyright holders, Quarto would like to apologize for any omissions.

Author Acknowledgments

Thanks go to Quarto for giving me this opportunity, especially my new friend Sarah Vickery who was great fun and very patient. Also, my good friend Luise Roberts who made it all possible and fed me at the same time. A very big thank you to David Crawford for letting me use lots of his stunning, inspirational photography.

And, finally thanks to my wife Lesley for inspiring, encouraging, understanding and typing!